"For the person whose loved one has anxiety, or for the pe himself or herself, Kate N. Thieda's book is practical and Especially reassuring is that the author blames no one, nor does she claim to teach the reader how to 'fix' anyone. She offers both understanding of the anxious behavior and tools to change one's response to it."

> —**Kristi Webb, PsyD**, licensed psychologist, DBT therapist, and a specialist in depression, anxiety, and trauma

"As an anxiety disorder specialist, I frequently see my clients' loved ones at their wits' end—not knowing what to do, how to help, or how to cope. If your loved one suffers from anxiety, I strongly encourage you to read this book."

> —**Julie Pike, PhD**, licensed psychologist and expert in the treatment of anxiety disorders

"This is a very easy-to-read book that provides a clear understanding of the ways that anxiety affects relationships. As Kate N. Thieda points out, good communication is critical in any successful relationship—and especially one that is hampered by anxiety. This book presents readers with important information on how to use effective communication strategies and other techniques for improving relationships impacted by these problems."

> —**Jonathan S. Abramowitz, PhD, ABPP**, professor and associate chair of psychology at the University of North Carolina (UNC) at Chapel Hill, director of the UNC Anxiety and Stress Disorders Clinic

"Countless clients with anxiety ask about a book that will teach their partners about anxiety and offer suggestions for how to help. At last, this is that book! With compassion and practicality, the author offers an understanding of how anxiety impacts a relationship, as well as excellent strategies for how to tackle anxiety and stay strong as a couple. This is a must-get book for anyone loving someone with anxiety."

> —**Annette R. Perot, PhD**, licensed psychologist specializing in the treatment of anxiety disorders

"A must-read for partners living with a love one experiencing any form of anxiety! Through both partners' eyes, Thieda provides robust and engaging content on the common thought patterns, reactions, and behaviors creating anxiety, along with reflective questions, exercises, interpersonal tools, and strategies for supporting loved ones. She skillfully incorporates mindfulness strategies (including affirmation and self-care) as enhancing practices for living in the present moment, dissolving anxiety, and promoting inner calmness. Kate's book is chock-full of helpful examples, insights, and resources for both partners!"

—**Judith C. Holder, PhD**, director at Duke Occupational Mental Health Programs, leadership and life coach-consultant, and author of *Mastering Life's Adventures: On the Beam*

The Loving Someone Series

If your loved one has a psychological disorder, you want to do everything you can to help them feel loved, supported, and safe. However, it's also important for you to establish personal boundaries so that you can avoid becoming overwhelmed.

New Harbinger's *Loving Someone Series* was developed to help readers like you truly understand a loved one's disorder, the medication or treatments that are available, and how to take care of your own needs so that you don't lose yourself in the process. As the family member or partner of someone with mental illness, you face your own set of unique challenges. Our books can provide powerful, evidence-based tools to help both you and your loved one live happier, healthier lives.

For a complete list of books in this series,
visit **newharbinger.com**

loving someone

with
anxiety

Understanding &
Helping Your Partner

KATE N. THIEDA, MS, LPCA

New Harbinger Publications, Inc.

Publisher's Note

This publication is designed to provide accurate and authoritative information in regard to the subject matter covered. It is sold with the understanding that the publisher is not engaged in rendering psychological, financial, legal, or other professional services. If expert assistance or counseling is needed, the services of a competent professional should be sought.

Distributed in Canada by Raincoast Books

Copyright © 2013 by Kate N. Thieda

New Harbinger Publications, Inc.
5674 Shattuck Avenue
Oakland, CA 94609
www.newharbinger.com

Cover design by Amy Shoup; Acquired by Melissa Kirk;
Edited by Jasmine Star

Library of Congress Cataloging-in-Publication Data

Thieda, Kate.
  Loving someone with anxiety : understanding and helping your partner / Kate Thieda, MS, LCPA.
      pages cm. -- (The New Harbinger loving someone series)
  Includes bibliographical references.
  ISBN 978-1-60882-611-7 (pbk. : alk. paper) -- ISBN 978-1-60882-612-4 (pdf e-book)-- ISBN 978-1-60882-613-1 (epub) 1. Anxiety. 2. Couples--Psychology. 3. Interpersonal relations. I. Title.
  BF575.A6T48 2013
  152.4'6--dc23

                          2012047225

Printed in the United States of America

15   14   13

10   9   8   7   6   5   4   3   2   1

First printing

Contents

Introduction

Loving someone with anxiety can be both tiring and frustrating. It may seem as though no matter what you do or say, it's never enough to help your partner relax and feel safe. You may find yourself living a lifestyle that you never intended because you're accommodating your partner's anxiety. Whether your partner has the kind of "everyday" anxiety that all humans experience or struggles with a diagnosable anxiety disorder, this book can help.

Do any of the following situations sound familiar?

- Do you constantly reassure your partner that the worst-case scenario is not actually going to happen?

- Do you participate in rituals with your partner that seem strange or unnecessary, such as washing your hands a certain number of times a day, arranging items in the pantry or closet "just so," counting objects or steps, or checking the door locks and windows numerous times before leaving the house or going to bed?

- Do you take on responsibilities that your partner once handled because she's unable to leave the house or afraid something will happen if she does?

- Do you check areas where your partner will be ahead of time for feared objects, such as snakes or insects?

- Are your activities with your partner limited by a need to avoid elevators, heights, air travel, and so on, because of your partner's fear?

- Do you feel helpless when your partner has a panic attack?

- Do you call your partner's supervisor to make excuses about why he isn't at work when the real reason is that he's too anxious to go?

- Do you walk on eggshells so as not to trigger anxiety in your partner?

- Do you avoid intimacy because your partner has insecurities about her body?

- Do you wonder if your relationship can survive your partner's anxiety?

If you said yes to any of these questions, you are not alone. Anxiety is one of the most prevalent mental disorders in the United States. An estimated 18.1 percent of American adults experience the effects of anxiety disorders each year (Kessler et al. 2005). Based on the current population of the United States, that's about forty-three million people. Even more people have anxiety that doesn't meet the criteria for an official diagnosis but impacts their lives nevertheless. When you add in partners, family members, and friends whose lives are touched by the anxiety of those they love, the number of people whose quality of life is impaired by anxiety skyrockets. In addition, not everyone seeks professional treatment for anxiety, which can cause needless suffering for both them and their loved ones.

This book is filled with practical explanations, examples, exercises, and advice that will allow you to help your partner with his anxiety and keep your relationship and your own sanity intact in the process. The emphasis is on working together as a couple to resolve issues in your relationship that may be fueling anxiety. However, I also recommend that you seek help from a trained mental health professional, as specialized treatment can be crucial for recovery, especially with certain anxiety disorders. In addition, anxiety often co-occurs with other mental health issues, including depression, substance abuse, and eating disorders, making professional treatment all the more important. Your support is an essential part of your partner's recovery from anxiety, and your knowledge and understanding of what's happening for your partner may make recovery easier.

How This Book Will Help

In reading this book, you may be looking for ways to help your partner overcome her anxiety. You definitely will learn strategies and lifestyle changes that can reduce the negative effects of anxiety on your relationship, but this isn't a step-by-step manual for "fixing" your partner. Instead, we'll focus on ways you can work together as a couple to better understand what anxiety is, how it's affecting your relationship, and what steps you can take to improve your lives.

Chapter 1 explains the difference between "everyday" anxiety and the six anxiety disorders currently diagnosed by mental health professionals. It includes case examples that illustrate what each anxiety disorder looks like in real life and discusses the thoughts and behaviors that anxious people contend with on a daily basis. Chapter 1 wraps up with an explanation of medications and therapy approaches used to reduce or eliminate anxiety.

The focus of chapter 2 is on how anxiety impacts romantic relationships, including effects on work and home responsibilities, socializing, sex, and parenting. While you may have realized that your partner's anxiety has changed the shape of your relationship, taking time to assess the ways both of you have learned to accommodate the anxiety may be eye-opening. You and your partner may discover that your lives are controlled by anxiety, rather than you controlling it.

Chapter 3 is specifically for you as the supportive partner of an anxious person. The writing exercises in this chapter invite you to explore your feelings around your partner's anxiety. For many people, these feelings include frustration, anger, loneliness, sadness, guilt, and—yes—anxiety. Taking the time to focus on your reactions to your partner's anxiety will help you identify opportunities for you and your partner to make changes. This chapter also introduces the idea of accommodation and how seemingly helpful behaviors can actually make an anxiety problem worse.

Chapters 4, 5, and 6 dive in to the challenges of communication and strategies for coping with and reducing anxiety. All three chapters offer a lot of practical advice and many effective techniques. Communication is a tough topic for most couples, whether or not anxiety is an issue. Therefore, chapter 4 focuses on skills for effective communication and suggests ways to practice these techniques when communicating with your partner, whether to resolve an issue that's come up between you or because you need to broach a difficult topic and don't want to generate needless anxiety. Once you've learned these techniques, chapters 5 and 6 will help you and your partner decide how best to respond when anxiety is present.

Chapter 7 explains some lifestyle changes that can help to decrease the impact of anxiety. You and your partner may not have given much thought to how certain foods and beverages, lack of exercise, technology, and media can increase your partner's anxiety. The information you learn in this chapter will challenge you to take charge of your lifestyle and think and act differently.

Finally, chapter 8, like chapter 3, is specifically for you. Being a caregiver is hard work, and you may feel as though you aren't getting a lot of support. Therefore, this chapter discusses how you can take care of your mind and body so that you aren't in danger of caregiver burnout.

My hope is that once you have read this book you'll feel knowledgeable about your partner's experience with anxiety, and that you'll also feel prepared to handle the variety of sticky situations that anxiety can create in your relationship. I also hope that it will help you be mindful of your own thoughts and feelings and support you in your own self-care. Your partner is lucky to have someone who cares enough about his or her well-being to commit to reading a book about anxiety. If the two of you work together as a team, you will notice positive changes in your lives and relationship.

CHAPTER 1

Understanding Anxiety and How It's Treated

Everyone has anxiety. Who hasn't experienced a racing heart, sweaty palms, a jumpy stomach, shortness of breath, trouble sleeping, restlessness, or a mind that just won't quiet down? Anxiety is a normal occurrence that alerts the brain and body that something isn't right. It would actually be detrimental if we didn't experience anxiety on occasion, because then we might not react appropriately to genuine threats to our safety or well-being.

Even though everyone is subject to occasional anxiety, it can be difficult to watch a loved one struggle with excessive anxiety that clearly interferes with his enjoyment of life. You undoubtedly want the best for your partner, and seeing him be so affected by his worries can be wearing. Plus, it can be difficult to protect the relationship and your own quality of life from negative impacts due to your partner's anxieties. This can lead to frustration, anger, sadness, guilt, loneliness, and more. In addition, you may feel sympathy for your partner and overextend yourself in efforts to alleviate his anxiety. Perhaps you feel pressured to make everything "just right" but also feel as though you'll never be able to stay one step ahead in preventing or even figuring out what might trigger anxiety for your partner. You may have known all along that your partner had a tendency to be anxious, but living with the effects of that anxiety every day takes a toll.

By reading this book, you're taking steps toward getting a better handle on what's going on with your anxious partner and how you can improve your relationship so that anxiety isn't the focus. No one wants a relationship where every decision is made on the basis of the other person's anxiety. Anxiety puts a lot of limits on life. You and your partner deserve better.

What Is Anxiety?

While we don't know exactly what causes anxiety, we do know that the capacity to feel anxious is biologically hardwired into us. Some people are more susceptible to feeling anxious than others, but as yet there isn't a definitive biological explanation for this. In addition, how people react to anxiety is a combination of many factors, including genetics, life history, self-esteem, past exposure to stress and trauma, current medical and psychological conditions, and previous experience handling stress, to name just a few. As a result, anxiety is a highly subjective experience, meaning each person feels it uniquely. What may trigger only a mildly anxious feeling in one person can result in a full-blown panic attack in another.

Anxiety is considered an emotion, and like most emotions, it can vary in intensity. At low levels, anxiety is adaptive, meaning that it drives positive outcomes, such as encouraging you to pay your bills on time or to work a few extra hours in order to meet a deadline. Higher anxiety levels, on the other hand, can set off a chain of events that can have significant negative physical and psychological effects. One thing that distinguishes adaptive, "everyday" anxiety from more problematic anxiety and diagnosable anxiety disorders is whether the anxiety resolves when the stressful situation is over or continues even in the absence of an imminent threat. I'll discuss this distinction in detail later in this chapter. For now, let's take a closer look at common anxiety symptoms and what those signs mean.

Common Anxiety Symptoms

Although the experience of anxiety is highly individualized, certain physical, behavioral, and emotional symptoms are common, as are certain thought patterns. As you read the following sections, think about whether you've observed any of these signs in your partner when he's feeling anxious.

Physical Signs of Anxiety

Common physical symptoms of anxiety include a racing heart, excessive perspiration, trembling or shaking, feeling restless or keyed up, fatigue or problems sleeping, shortness of breath, chest pain or tightness, nausea or diarrhea, upset stomach or butterflies in the stomach, dizziness, chills or hot flushes, and numbness. Another physical sign is an exaggerated response when startled, like jumping a mile if someone says something to you from behind when you didn't know anyone was there. It's important to note that these symptoms are natural responses to normal anxiety and don't necessarily mean someone has an anxiety disorder. Rather, the severity, duration, and effects of these symptoms are key factors in determining whether people are experiencing an anxiety disorder or just a typical response to anxiety.

Behavioral Signs of Anxiety

How your partner acts when he's experiencing anxiety can offer a lot of clues about what's going on for him internally. Some common behaviors of people who are anxious include avoiding places or events that trigger anxiety, such as bridges, elevators, or parties; fleeing situations that make them uncomfortable, such as a movie theater or crowded restaurant; performing compulsive behaviors repeatedly, such as washing their hands time and time again or checking the door locks a precise number of times before going to bed; limiting outside activities by not leaving home or only going to a few specific "safe" places; and engaging in risky, self-destructive behaviors, such as drinking or taking drugs. Ironically, even though your partner may feel as if these behaviors reduce his anxiety, they actually make it worse.

Emotional Signs of Anxiety

As mentioned, anxiety is an emotion, and it can evoke a lot of different feelings. Common words your partner might use when trying to describe his experience of anxiety are "worry," "apprehension," "fear," "dread," "uneasiness," "distress," "feeling overwhelmed," "panic," "pressure," "terror," "jumpiness," "stress," and "edginess." Your partner may also say he can't describe what he's feeling or might simply say, "Something isn't right." These emotional responses to anxiety often arise due to thought patterns common among people with anxiety, so let's take a look at those.

Common Thoughts That Signal Anxiety

The thoughts people experience when feeling anxious are commonly referred to as "worry" (Bourne 2005). Everyone worries sometimes, but people who are experiencing persistent anxiety have more worry thoughts than typical and struggle to think of other things. Here are some common worry thoughts:

- *What if _____ happens?*

- *I can't cope with this.*

- *I'll never be able to handle _____.*

- *This is too much for me. I'm going to fail.*

- *I have to be in control.*

- *I might as well give up now. This isn't going to work, no matter how hard I try.*

- *Everyone is going to laugh at me.*

- *I must be going crazy!*

Again, people can have these thoughts and *not* have an anxiety disorder. To understand the distinction, let's take a look at the difference between "everyday" anxiety and a diagnosable anxiety disorder.

"Everyday" Anxiety vs. Anxiety Disorders

It can be a fine line to distinguish between "everyday" anxiety and a diagnosable condition. Often the distinction hinges on whether people describe symptoms of anxiety that interfere with their quality of life, are pervasive, and negatively impact their performance (whether that's in one area of life or across all situations).

For example, if your partner has a big presentation coming up at work soon and has been working extremely hard to pull it together, he might be feeling anxious. Symptoms of that anxiety might include

Worry or Rumination?

Both worry and rumination are persistent forms of negative thinking. Worry thoughts are fixated on the what-ifs of the future, while rumination involves being consumed with unpleasant thoughts about past events. Another difference between the two is that worry is usually focused on danger, whereas rumination is entangled with hopelessness, failure, and loss. People who ruminate have a higher risk of depression.

having trouble sleeping, being irritable and impatient, and having worry thoughts about what might go wrong. This could be "everyday" anxiety, or it could be a sign of an anxiety disorder, depending on how long the symptoms have been going on, the severity of the symptoms, and whether they resolve after he gives the presentation. If his symptoms do go away afterward, he was probably experiencing "everyday" anxiety in response to a stressful situation. If he still struggles with his symptoms afterward and also feels anxious about other life situations, it might be a sign of an anxiety disorder.

Aaron Beck, an eminent psychiatrist and early developer of cognitive therapy, describes people with anxiety disorders as having a "hypersensitive alarm system" (Beck and Emery 2005, 31). In his view, they are so sensitive to any stimuli that might indicate imminent danger that they constantly warn themselves about potential danger. Unfortunately, almost any stimulus can trip the alarm, and as a result, they are in a constant state of anxiety.

It's estimated that over forty-three million Americans have an anxiety disorder (Kessler et al. 2005), or almost one in five adults. So whether or not your partner has been diagnosed with an anxiety disorder, he's far from alone: many others have similar difficulties with anxiety. The good news is that anxiety disorders are among the most treatable mental health conditions. The possibly not-so-good news is that many people choose not to consult a mental health professional about their symptoms and suffer needlessly as a result.

In the following sections, I'll describe the major anxiety disorders. If your partner has been diagnosed with an anxiety disorder, the discussion of that disorder may give you more insight into what your partner is experiencing. If your partner doesn't have a diagnosis, please understand that this information shouldn't be used to attempt to diagnose your partner; only a trained mental health professional can do that. Nevertheless, even if your partner hasn't been diagnosed or doesn't qualify for an official diagnosis of an anxiety disorder, this discussion—and this book—will still be relevant and helpful.

Types of Anxiety Disorders

The American Psychiatric Association (2000) has identified six types of anxiety disorders:

- Generalized anxiety disorder

- Obsessive-compulsive disorder

- Panic disorder

- Post-traumatic stress disorder

- Social phobia or social anxiety disorder

- Specific phobias

Each of these disorders is diagnosed by trained mental health professionals using criteria outlined by the American Psychiatric Association in the *Diagnostic and Statistical Manual of Mental Disorders* (2000). As you'll learn, there are overlaps in the criteria for these disorders, but also characteristics that make each condition distinct. In addition, it isn't uncommon for people to be diagnosed with multiple anxiety disorders or to have another mental disorder along with an anxiety disorder. (Having two or more diagnosable mental or physical health conditions is referred to as comorbidity.)

In addition to describing each of the six anxiety disorders in the following sections, I've also provided brief real-life examples.

Generalized Anxiety Disorder

Linda is a forty-seven-year-old proprietor of a small business. She feels like she's constantly worrying about everything: Is her business making enough money? Will she and her partner, Bill, be able to pay for their daughter's college tuition? Is her fatigue just because of working too much, or does she have some mysterious disease? What if her taxes are audited? What will she and Bill do if their house suddenly needs a major repair? Despite knowing that many of her fears are unfounded, Linda struggles to control her thoughts and relax. Bill does his best to relieve her worries, reassuring her that everything is fine and nothing bad will happen, but it seems like no matter what he says, it's never enough.

Linda is a typical example of someone who might be diagnosed with generalized anxiety disorder (GAD). People who have GAD tend to go through life chronically worried, even though there's little or no basis for their concern. People with GAD anticipate disaster and worry excessively about things that probably will never happen. Concerns about money, illness, relationships, or work problems dominate their thoughts. For some, the thought of just getting through the day can be overwhelming. People with GAD usually realize that their concerns are excessive, but they still struggle to let go of their worry thoughts. In addition, people with GAD often have a comorbid disorder, such as another anxiety disorder, depression, an eating disorder, or substance abuse.

People with mild GAD can usually hold down jobs, take care of their daily responsibilities for the most part, and have typical social relationships. Those with more severe GAD may have trouble with everyday tasks. Avoiding specific activities or situations, such as riding an elevator or driving, isn't a symptom of GAD; rather, these are specific phobias, which I'll describe shortly.

GAD usually develops gradually. It can appear at any point in a person's life but is most commonly diagnosed between childhood and middle age. Genetics may play a role in whether a person has a predisposition toward developing GAD, and women are twice as likely as men to be diagnosed with GAD (Robins and Regier 1991).

Obsessive-Compulsive Disorder

Emily is a thirty-six-year-old mother of two small children. She finds herself having the urgent need to wash her hands many, many times a day, especially after playing with her kids outside, going out in public with them, or doing something that seems dirty to her. If she's able to wash her hands exactly twenty-eight times, she feels better...until the next time she encounters something that might have germs on it. Her hands are chapped and often bleed from the excessive washing, but she feels unable to reduce the number of times she washes. Her partner, Sarah, has expressed concern about Emily's need to wash her hands constantly but hasn't been able to persuade Emily to stop.

Emily's urgent, uncontrollable need to wash her hands excessively is a result of her struggle with obsessive-compulsive disorder (OCD). People with OCD have obsessions: distressing, recurring thoughts that compel them to perform rituals (compulsions) in order to relieve their distress. Unfortunately, these rituals usually end up controlling the person, making things worse instead of better. Performing the rituals isn't pleasurable, but those with OCD often feel as if they have no other option for relieving the anxiety associated with their obsessions.

It's common for people to joke that they have OCD because they're rigid about how they do certain things, such as following a set routine in the morning because they fear that if they don't, they'll forget to do something or be late for work. The difference between a ritual that isn't obsessive and one that's driven by OCD is that people with OCD become extremely upset and are often unable to function if they can't perform the ritual. Rituals overtake their lives, whereas those who don't have OCD can adapt and go on with their day even if their routines are disturbed.

Contamination fears and compulsive hand washing are just one example of how OCD manifests. Other common examples are a person who is obsessed about safety and, as a result, locks, relocks, and checks all the doors and windows in the house over and over again before going to sleep at night or repeatedly checks things that might pose a danger, such as whether the stove is turned off or the iron unplugged. Some people with OCD get relief from their obsessions by touching things, particularly in a certain sequence, or by mentally counting objects or numbers repeatedly. Other common symptoms of OCD are a need for symmetry or order, difficulty throwing things away, and hoarding.

OCD can become a severe problem that prevents people from being able to function in a work environment or live safely at home. People with OCD commonly have comorbid disorders, such as other anxiety disorders, an eating disorder, or depression. They may also take excessive measures to avoid triggering situations or use alcohol or drugs in an effort to calm their anxiety. The prevalence of OCD is nearly equal in women and men (Robins and Regier 1991).

Panic Disorder

Mike is a twenty-seven-year-old graduate student preparing to take his comprehensive exams. Understandably, he's having some anxiety, since whether or not he passes determines whether he will graduate. But one night something weird happened: As he sat down to study, he suddenly felt light-headed, started to sweat profusely, had chest pain, and couldn't breathe. This episode lasted about ten minutes, and Mike thought he was going crazy, having a heart attack, or both. His partner, Michelle, didn't know what to do or how to help him, but Mike insisted she not call for help. When the episode was over, Michelle took Mike to the urgent care clinic, and the tests they ran came back negative for physical issues. Now Mike is worried that it will happen again, not just because it was really scary, but also because of how embarrassing it would be if it happened at school or in public and others witnessed it.

Mike had a panic attack when sitting down to study for his exam. Panic attacks occur without warning and are characterized by sudden feelings of terror accompanied by a racing heart, excessive sweating, weakness, and feeling faint or dizzy. Other symptoms include numbness or tingling in the hands, feeling flushed or chilled, chest pain, feeling nauseated, and having the sensation of being unable to breathe. As a result of these symptoms, people who are having a panic attack often believe they are having a heart attack, losing their mind, or about to die. The reality is that, despite how panic attacks mimic heart attack symptoms, they aren't fatal (though an extreme reaction to a panic attack may sometimes lead to serious injury or possibly even death). Panic attacks can happen at any time, even when people are asleep. They usually peak within ten minutes and subside naturally, but some symptoms can linger much longer.

A key symptom of panic disorder is the fear that a panic attack will occur again. Many people who have a single panic attack never have another one, but others develop panic disorder and have panic attacks repeatedly. The tendency to develop panic disorder appears to be hereditary. Panic disorder is diagnosed twice as often in women as in men (Robins and Regier 1991).

Panic Attack or "Crazy Worry"?

Your partner may be describing his experience of intense anxiety as panic attacks when, in reality, a better name for what he's experiencing would be "crazy worry." Here are some key differences between a true panic attack and "crazy worry":

- Panic attacks are usually short in duration, peaking in ten minutes or so and then subsiding. "Crazy worry" can go on for hours, days, or even weeks or months.

- Panic attack symptoms, while similar to "crazy worry" symptoms, tend to be more intense. During a panic attack, people may feel as if they are having a heart attack, going crazy, or dying. "Crazy worry" symptoms are generally tolerable even though they're really uncomfortable. People call ambulances for panic attacks; it's less likely that would happen for someone experiencing "crazy worry."

- "Crazy worry" usually occurs in response to a stressor. Panic attacks come out of the blue and may not be associated with anything in particular.

People who develop panic disorder often become restricted in their daily lives because of their fear of having a panic attack. This can develop into agoraphobia, a fear of being in situations where escape would be difficult. If a panic attack occurs in a specific place, people may develop a specific phobia related to that place and become restricted in what they can do because of the specific phobia. For example, a panic attack in an elevator that leads to a specific phobia about elevators could restrict where a person might live, work, visit friends and family, or access services. Some people with panic disorder can only go out in public if they have a trusted person with them, which also severely limits their quality of life.

Post-Traumatic Stress Disorder

George is a twenty-one-year-old man who has served two tours of duty in war zones. Since returning from his second deployment, he's been having difficulty settling in at home and reestablishing a normal life with his girlfriend, Kristy. He's having trouble sleeping, and when he does manage to sleep, he often has distressing dreams about combat and seeing people die. When he's awake, he's easily startled by loud noises or by Kristy "surprising" him when he didn't know she was in the room. Sometimes he has flashbacks, which make him feel as if he is back in combat, seeing, hearing, and smelling everything just as it was when he was deployed. Kristy gets frightened when this happens because it's as if George loses touch with reality. In addition, George often has angry outbursts and feels the need to be vigilant about keeping himself safe, even though he knows he isn't in a war zone any longer.

George has post-traumatic stress disorder (PTSD). Although the media has given a lot of coverage to veterans who are suffering from PTSD as a result of military experience, PTSD can develop from any traumatic event, including being raped, mugged, or assaulted; being kidnapped or abused; being in a car accident or plane crash; experiencing a bombing or fire; or living through a natural disaster, such as an earthquake, flood, or tornado. The triggering event may have happened to the person, to a loved one, or in the person's presence, such as witnessing someone else being harmed.

Common symptoms that indicate PTSD are the inability to feel a range of emotions, distancing from others, being easily startled, avoiding situations that could trigger memories, being hypervigilant, having trouble sleeping, being aggressive or irritable, having trouble with intimacy, and sometimes being violent toward others. Anniversaries of the triggering event are often very difficult. PTSD symptoms may be more severe when the event was purposely perpetuated by another person, such as in a rape, mugging, or kidnapping (National Institute of Mental Health [NIMH] 2009).

People with PTSD often relive their experience, both while awake and while asleep. The waking memories are called flashbacks, and the person may not realize that the flashback isn't reality. Flashbacks can be triggered by ordinary stimuli, such as a door slamming or a car horn honking. During a flashback, images, sounds, smells, and feelings from the triggering event can all be present. When sleeping, the person may have disturbing nightmares about the event.

In order to be diagnosed with PTSD, the symptoms must be present for at least four weeks. Not every person who experiences a traumatic event will develop PTSD, and research indicates that women are twice as likely to develop PTSD as men (Breslau 2002). The duration of PTSD varies from person to person. Some people recover quickly, whereas for others it becomes a chronic condition. As with the other anxiety disorders, PTSD often isn't the only psychiatric condition a person has. Depression, substance abuse, and other anxiety disorders often also afflict those with PTSD.

Social Phobia or Social Anxiety Disorder

Jane is a fifty-three-year-old executive assistant at a large corporation. She's held her position for over twenty years but frequently worries that she'll be fired. Despite having consistently positive job performance reviews throughout her career, Jane cringes when her boss or coworkers say anything about her work, even if their comments aren't critical. In addition, she struggles to make small talk with her colleagues, preferring to work alone in the safety of her office with the door closed. She rarely accepts invitations to lunch or to socialize outside of work out of fear that her coworkers will discover "the real Jane"—one who isn't worthy of being liked. Jane is convinced that if she were to lose her job, she would never be hired elsewhere. Jane's husband, Elliot, has been listening to Jane's worries about her job performance for the twenty-five years he's known her. At this point, he mostly tunes her out when she starts worrying out loud because he's learned that nothing he says or does helps her feel better.

Jane's concerns about her job performance are an example of the struggles those with social phobia experience. This disorder is diagnosed when a person experiences such intense and overwhelming anxiety and self-consciousness in the presence of others that it interferes with relationships. Those who have social phobia live with constant fear of being observed and judged by others or doing something embarrassing. This fear is so pervasive that some people with social phobia worry about encounters with others for days or weeks ahead of time. This can prevent them from being successful at school and work and in creating and maintaining relationships.

Social phobia may be limited to certain situations, such as talking or eating in front of others, or it may be broader in scope, where any activity involving people other than a small, trusted circle causes paralyzing anxiety. Here are some situations that those with social phobia commonly fear:

- Public speaking or performing

- Making small talk

- Participating in group discussions

- Asking questions while in a group

- Being introduced to new people

- Meeting or talking with strangers

- Being assertive

- Being watched while doing something, such as eating or writing

- Attending social gatherings

- Using the telephone

- Using public restrooms

- Interacting with "important" people, such as supervisors, people in authority, or people with high social standing or power

- Being evaluated indirectly, such as when taking a test

People with social phobia usually recognize that their fears about scrutiny from others are overblown but feel powerless to change their thoughts. Social phobia is different from shyness in that people with social phobia don't experience relief once the dreaded situation is in progress, whereas people who are simply shy often feel better once they're in the situation because they're able to get comfortable and warm up to it. People with social phobia, on the other hand, continue to feel intense anxiety when in the situation and will obsess over the interaction long after it is over, analyzing their performance and what others might have thought about them.

Social phobia generally develops in childhood or adolescence and affects women and men equally (Bourdon et al. 1988). Many people with social phobia self-medicate by using alcohol or drugs prior to a social engagement in order to "calm down," which can lead to substance dependence or abuse.

Specific Phobias

John is a twenty-six-year-old national sales executive for a financial firm. He works ten- to twelve-hour days, spending a lot of time on the phone and driving to meet with clients in an effort to close deals. He tells himself and others that he enjoys the pace, and actually does feel that he thrives on the challenges the job offers. But when he has to fly to a meeting across the country, he experiences sweaty palms, a rapid heartbeat, racing thoughts, and a feeling that he's losing it. As a result, he has started avoiding taking on clients in locations that might require travel by plane. In addition, his partner, Matt, loves to travel, but John has made excuse after excuse about why they can't take a trip together, which is both disappointing and frustrating to Matt.

John is experiencing a specific phobia. Specific phobias are intense, irrational fears of something that doesn't actually pose a threat. People who have specific phobias are usually aware that their fears are irrational, but they're unable to talk themselves out of their reaction to the triggering situation. For some, just thinking about the feared object or situation is enough to bring on severe anxiety.

Common specific phobias involve flying, heights, elevators, enclosed places, animals or insects, blood or needles, water, bridges, and storms. Something interesting about specific phobias is how very specific they can be. For example, someone may be able to hike up a mountain and look over the landscape below with no problem but be terrified of going above the third floor of an office building.

Specific phobias can cause problems by restricting people's lives in a variety of ways. Someone who has a fear of driving over bridges, for example, probably won't take a job that involves a commute over a bridge. A person with a fear of blood may avoid needed medical or dental procedures. Someone with a fear of dogs may panic if a dog approaches and run into traffic while trying to escape.

Phobias often develop in childhood, but they can appear at any time. Unless the person receives treatment, the phobia tends to persist. Specific phobias are twice as common in women as men (Bourdon et al. 1988). While it's unclear exactly what causes specific phobias to develop, they generally respond well to targeted exposure therapy, which I'll discuss in detail in chapter 6.

Anxiety in Women vs. Men

As you probably noticed when reading the sections about the different anxiety disorders, women are diagnosed with many of them more frequently than men are. To review, women are twice as likely as men to have GAD, panic disorder, PTSD, or specific phobias and are equally as likely to be diagnosed with OCD or social phobia. In addition, anxiety disorders are more common among women who didn't complete high school or college than among men with the same level of education (Kessler et al. 1995).

Despite these startling numbers, little is known about why women are more likely to develop anxiety disorders. There are, however, several hypotheses, including causes such as genetic influences, early exposure to physical or sexual abuse (which is more typical for girls than boys), early exposure to stressful events, and the effects of women's menstrual cycles (Shear et al. 2005). What does all of this mean if your partner is female? Here are some of the findings:

- Your partner is not only more likely to have an anxiety disorder, but also more likely to have a comorbid disorder, such as depression or alcohol or drug abuse (Kessler et al. 2002).

- Panic disorder is often more severe in women than in men. Among women, panic disorder is also associated with higher levels of comorbid psychiatric illnesses, such as agoraphobia and GAD (Pigott 1999; Turgeon, Marchand, and Dupuis 1998).

- Women who have been assaulted are nearly three times more likely to develop PTSD than men who have had a similar experience. Women with PTSD often have symptoms of avoidance and numbing, whereas men report difficulties with impulse control and irritability (Breslau 2002).

- Women with social anxiety disorder may be at greater risk for agoraphobia than men (Pigott 1999).

- Women with OCD are more likely to have obsessions and compulsions related to cleaning, contamination, or checking, or to have co-occurring depression or eating disorders, but also symptoms that are, overall, less severe than those of men (Pigott 1999).

- There is evidence that anxiety improves during pregnancy, particularly during the third trimester. However, small studies have indicated that, once the baby is born, panic disorder and OCD are exacerbated, which can lead to an increase of OCD behaviors, as well as depression (Cohen et al. 1994).

Conversely, men are diagnosed with anxiety disorders less frequently than women, and there are several theories about why this discrepancy exists. One is that men are often misdiagnosed when they go to their doctors with symptoms of anxiety disorders. Other theories are that men are more likely to self-medicate with drugs or alcohol, or that men tend to avoid seeking treatment because of cultural biases that anxiety is unacceptable for men. Nevertheless, it also appears that men genuinely are not as prone to anxiety as women are—and, again, the reasons for this remain unknown. However, a recent study at Florida State University indicated that men's higher levels of testosterone might play a role in reducing anxiety levels (Hartung 2010).

Treatments for Anxiety Disorders

While it's helpful to understand anxiety, the distinctions between different anxiety disorders, and gender differences in the prevalence of anxiety, you probably have a more pressing question: How is anxiety treated? There are many approaches, and later chapters in this book will introduce you and your partner to a variety of techniques for reducing or eliminating anxiety that don't involve medication or psychotherapy. But sometimes professional treatment for anxiety is the most effective approach, so let's take a look at what that might mean for your partner. The good news is that anxiety usually responds quickly to effective treatment.

In general, when people seek help from mental health professionals for anxiety disorders, they receive recommendations for specific types of talk therapy and/or psychiatric medications. The type of treatment that's appropriate is specific to the person; what may work for one person may not be effective for another. The diagnosing professional must take a careful history to determine the origins of the anxiety and particularly whether it's a psychological or physical problem, as some physical illnesses can cause symptoms similar to those of anxiety but the symptoms will resolve when the physical illness is treated. If professionals determine that an anxiety disorder is present, they also look for comorbid disorders, such as depression, drug and/or alcohol abuse, or another anxiety disorder.

In the rest of this chapter, I'll discuss the most common medications and types of therapy recommended for anxiety. In addition, you and your partner may consider complementary and alternative medicine (CAM) therapies. Unfortunately, studies looking at the effectiveness of psychiatric medications and psychological therapies for treating anxiety vastly outnumber those examining the effectiveness of CAM approaches (Antonacci et al. 2010), so these treatments are generally only recommended either in conjunction with standard therapies or if standard therapies haven't worked well. CAM options include exercise, acupuncture, herbal supplements, and relaxation techniques, and I'll cover some of these approaches in chapters 5, 6, and 7. Should your partner decide to try CAM options, it's a good idea to inform his doctor about everything he's trying to ensure all of the treatments are compatible. For example, some supplements can have problematic interactions with prescription medications. Keeping his doctor informed is also important in the event that your partner develops a medical problem.

Medications for Anxiety Disorders

Common types of medication prescribed for anxiety disorders include antianxiety drugs, antidepressants, and beta-blockers. These medications can help control symptoms, but they don't eradicate the anxiety disorder in the same way that an antibiotic would get rid of an infection. That's why psychotherapy is often recommended in conjunction with medication: People need to learn techniques for working with anxiety-related thoughts and practice coping skills that can help relieve anxiety symptoms.

If your partner is considering medications to relieve his anxiety, it's imperative that his doctor be aware of all other medicines he's taking, prescription or over-the-counter, as well as any vitamins, herbs, or other supplements. In addition, it's important to be honest about using illicit drugs or alcohol because of potentially fatal interactions.

ANTIANXIETY MEDICATIONS

Benzodiazepines are effective in managing anxiety symptoms. Commonly prescribed benzodiazepines include clonazepam (Klonopin) for social phobia and GAD, lorazepam (Ativan) for panic disorder, and alprazolam (Xanax) for panic disorder and GAD. In addition, a newer antianxiety medication, buspirone (Buspar), which is an azapirone, is used to treat GAD (NIMH 2009).

Benzodiazepines work quickly to relieve anxiety symptoms but can also result in dependence, meaning people need to take increasingly higher dosages to get the same results. Therefore, doctors generally only prescribe benzodiazepines for a short amount of time in order to prevent dependence. Buspirone, on the other hand, doesn't cause dependence, but it must be taken for approximately two weeks before the person will feel any effects.

ANTIDEPRESSANTS

Despite their name, some antidepressants have been shown to be effective in treating anxiety disorders, in addition to depression. Selective serotonin reuptake inhibitors (SSRIs) are the most commonly prescribed antidepressants today. They work by altering the levels of neurotransmitters in the brain, which affects communication among brain cells. According to the National Institute of Mental Health, "Fluoxetine (Prozac), sertraline (Zoloft), escitalopram (Lexapro), paroxetine (Paxil), and citalopram (Celexa) are some of the SSRIs commonly prescribed for panic disorder, OCD, PTSD, and social phobia. SSRIs are also used to treat panic disorder when it occurs in combination with OCD, social phobia, or depression. Venlafaxine (Effexor), a drug closely related to the SSRIs, is used to treat GAD. These medications are started at low doses and gradually increased until they have a beneficial effect" (NIMH 2009, 15).

Monoamine oxidase inhibitors (MAOIs) are the oldest type of antidepressants. MAOIs commonly prescribed for anxiety include phenelzine (Nardil), tranylcypromine (Parnate), and isocarboxazid (Marplan). These drugs have been shown to be effective in treating panic disorder and social phobia (NIMH 2009). However, MAOIs are not prescribed very frequently because taking them requires many dietary restrictions, and because they can cause dangerous side effects when combined with other medicines, such as pain relievers, birth control pills, herbal supplements, cold and allergy medications, and other antidepressants.

A third type of antidepressant, tricyclics, can also be helpful in treating anxiety disorders. Imipramine (Tofranil) is useful for treating panic disorder and GAD, and clomipramine (Anafranil) is helpful for OCD (NIMH 2009).

BETA-BLOCKERS

Beta-blockers were originally developed to treat heart conditions. However, they were subsequently found to be effective for some people in preventing the physical symptoms of anxiety, such as rapid heart rate and tremors. They are especially effective for symptoms of social phobia. A key benefit of taking a beta-blocker is that it helps assure people that their symptoms won't escalate, and this reduces the fear of something "disastrous" happening.

Psychotherapy for Anxiety

Psychotherapy is often recommended for treating anxiety disorders, sometimes in conjunction with medication and sometimes on its own. Psychotherapy is conducted by trained mental health professionals, including psychiatrists, psychologists, counselors, and social workers. The purpose of psychotherapy for anxiety disorders is to discover how the anxiety began and what triggers it and to help the person learn techniques to reduce, limit, or prevent anxiety.

Cognitive behavioral therapy (CBT) is especially helpful for anxiety. It's considered an evidence-based treatment, meaning extensive research has proven its effectiveness. The National Association of Cognitive-Behavioral Therapists defines CBT as "therapy that is based on the idea that our thoughts cause our feelings and behaviors, not external things, like people, situations, and events. The benefit of this fact is that we can change the way we think to feel/act better even if the situation does not change" (2011).

The cognitive part of CBT focuses on changing people's thoughts and feelings regarding their anxiety. That means the therapist and your partner will identify what those thoughts and feelings are, examine how they are affecting him, and then work to transform the thoughts and feelings so they no longer interfere with your partner's functioning and quality of life. The behavioral part of CBT looks at changing people's behaviors in response to their anxiety. Many CBT therapists also teach relaxation techniques and other coping skills to help manage anxiety symptoms. I'll explain several of these techniques in chapters 5, 6, and 7 so you and your partner can try them at home.

Treatment Failure

People often feel treatments for anxiety have failed when the actual problem is that the treatment hasn't been given enough time to work or the treatment is inappropriate for the problem. If your partner has previously tried treatment for his anxiety and it was unsuccessful, you may encounter some resistance about seeking professional help again. It is essential that he be honest with a new practitioner about previous attempts at treatment. This information can guide the practitioner in choosing a new and hopefully more effective treatment approach. Your partner also needs to advocate for himself and be honest about how he's responding to treatment. There are many options for treating anxiety, and it's usually possible to make adjustments until the person feels relief. If your partner is working with a treatment provider who's unwilling to listen to feedback about the treatment approach and make changes, he should seek out a new treatment provider.

In addition, you both need to have realistic expectations about what treatment can do. Psychoeducation about anxiety can help both of you learn about what to expect, what is "normal," and what has been proven to help. To achieve maximum benefits, it's imperative that your partner be active in his treatment. This includes following all instructions about when and how to take any prescribed medications, keeping appointments, and participating in psychotherapy, both in session and with homework assignments. Recovering from an anxiety disorder takes a lot of hard work, and having a supportive, understanding, and educated partner is extremely beneficial during that process.

What's Next?

After reading the descriptions of the six anxiety disorders in this chapter, you may have recognized your partner's symptoms as typical of one of the disorders. On the other hand, you may be thinking *Well, he doesn't quite fit any of the categories, but I know he has anxiety*. The truth is, it doesn't really matter whether your partner's anxiety is "diagnosable." If it's impairing your relationship or diminishing your partner's quality of life or your own quality of life, it will be worthwhile to make some changes. The rest of this book will give you tools and strategies to help your partner manage his anxiety and help both of you limit its impacts on your lives and relationship. Some of these techniques include writing exercises, so it would be helpful for you to have a journal handy as you read on.

CHAPTER 2

How Anxiety Affects Relationships

Anxiety affects nearly every aspect of a relationship. When you decided to enter into the relationship, you probably expected that your partner would be just that: a partner—someone who could communicate with you openly, who would accompany you to parties and events and on vacations, who would be your willing sexual partner, who would contribute financially to the relationship by having a job, and perhaps with whom you would have and raise children. Even if you were aware of your partner's anxiety at the outset, it might not have occurred to you that it could interfere with these dreams and expectations.

In 2004, Russell Research conducted a survey for the Anxiety Disorders Association of America (ADAA) that looked at how GAD affects relationships, including romantic relationships, friendships, and relationships in the workplace. The respondents included 530 people diagnosed with generalized anxiety disorder. The results probably won't surprise you: Most of the people with GAD indicated that anxiety had a significant effect on their relationships, and romantic relationships seemed to suffer most. Two-thirds of the people surveyed said they felt their romantic relationships would improve if they could eliminate their anxiety. I think it's safe to assume that those who suffer from any type of anxiety—whether it has a label or not—probably feel the same way.

This chapter will take a close look at how your partner's anxiety is affecting your relationship. At the end of each section, you'll find a short writing exercise to help you assess and evaluate how your relationship has been affected by your partner's anxiety, so grab your journal and a pen or pencil. Don't skip these exercises, as what you write will be useful later, when you read about how to make changes in your relationship to help reduce or eliminate your partner's anxiety.

Communication and Anxiety

Anyone who knows anything about romantic relationships will tell you that good communication between partners is essential. How else can you manage day-to-day responsibilities, make decisions, work out the challenges that arise, and simply let one another know how much you value each other and the relationship?

Unfortunately, your partner's anxiety can interfere with good communication. Depending on the severity of the anxiety and the circumstances in which your partner feels anxious, communication breakdowns may arise that can lead to serious consequences for your relationship. Your partner may have problems reacting appropriately to what you say, may have trouble expressing her feelings, or may misinterpret the meaning of what you say because she hears it through the filter of her anxiety—a filter that can twist a benign comment into something that was never intended and cause your partner to react in surprising or even baffling ways. She may also appear to be irritable, inflexible, or just plain rude for no good reason. If you find yourself wondering what you did to deserve such a reaction, what might actually be happening is that your partner is feeling anxious but can't express it.

How Communication Anxiety Can Affect Your Relationship

Your partner's anxiety affects her emotionally, and depending on how her feelings manifest, it may affect you as a result of seeing her experiencing those feelings. Some people with anxiety tend to suppress their feelings. Feelings in their full expression have a lot of power, and they can be scary, especially for people who grew up in an environment where it wasn't okay to have negative emotions, such as anger, sadness, or frustration.

By suppressing her feelings, your partner may be trying to maintain control over her world. In addition, she may try to keep her emotions inside because she's afraid of overwhelming you with them. This is especially likely if the feelings are negative. Your partner may feel anxious about hurting your feelings or damaging the relationship if "the truth"—whatever that is—comes out. The irony is that the more your partner denies herself the expression of her feelings, the more anxious she'll become. This is one reason why suppressed feelings can be overwhelming when they finally do surface.

On the other hand, it may seem as though the only thing your partner expresses is strong feelings. If so, this can be overwhelming for both of you and difficult to manage appropriately. If your partner isn't able to hold back her thoughts and feelings, you may often feel as if it's your responsibility to help alleviate whatever is triggering her anxiety. However, this can create negative thoughts and feelings for you, and "saving" your partner in this way isn't always the best idea, for reasons I'll explain in the next chapter.

Your partner may also feel that it's risky to express what she thinks or feels if she's unsure what the outcome of the conversation will be. Her anxiety has probably resulted in low confidence in her ability to support herself and her opinion, so she's likely to be concerned about what will happen if you don't understand her message or react negatively to what she has to say. She may need time to plan and rehearse what she wants to tell you and additional time to consider your response and continue the conversation. In chapter 4, you'll learn strategies to help the two of you communicate better, even when anxiety threatens to derail the conversation.

Another way that anxiety can affect communication is if your partner doesn't admit to her anxiety and instead acts irritable or rude or does something else to push you away. Avoidance probably seems easier than dealing with anxiety, and it can also help your partner feel as if she still has some control over the situation. As a result, she may try to derail the conversation, even if her behavior is out of character. People often don't realize that their irritability and avoidance behaviors are directly linked to their anxiety. All they know is that they feel uncomfortable, and therefore they react before considering their behavior. This makes it difficult to have a meaningful or effective conversation.

EXERCISE: Signs and Symptoms of Partner Anxiety

How do you know when your partner feels anxious about communicating with you? In your journal, make a list of the physical signals she gives, the words she tends to use, and the behaviors that indicate she's feeling anxious. You may want to refer back to the section "Common Anxiety Symptoms," in chapter 1, to help you identify the symptoms your partner displays.

Also think about how your partner's anxiety around communication has affected your relationship and write about this in your journal. List some specific instances when more effective communication between the two of you could have made a difference.

Anxiety in Social Settings

Being in social situations is often a huge issue for people with anxiety. They may avoid routine social situations that others think nothing of, such as going out for lunch or dinner with their partner or friends, making social phone calls, or attending family functions. They may also get anxious in day-to-day settings where other people are present, such as work environments, exercise facilities, and busy medical offices. For the purposes of this discussion, let's consider "social setting" to be any place where other people are present.

Two-thirds of the respondents in the ADAA survey of people with GAD said that they avoid some social situations (Russell Research 2004). This can lead to isolation and potential breakdown of relationships, and can also create a self-perpetuating cycle in which increased anxiety about others' thoughts and feelings and the status of relationships leads to more avoidance.

Although social anxiety disorder is one of the six diagnosable anxiety disorders, your partner need not meet the criteria for this disorder to be anxious in social settings. Many types of anxiety can affect how your partner feels in social settings.

Behaviors That Indicate Anxiety in Social Settings

Although your partner may act "normally" when at home or in other "safe" situations, in social situations her anxiety might turn her into someone you don't recognize. She may behave completely differently when she has to interact with others. For example, you may notice that she talks more, talks less or not at all, stutters, becomes tongue-tied when spoken to directly, or relies on you to drive conversations with other people. She may also show physical signs of discomfort, such as not making eye contact, fidgeting, playing with her hair or nails, blushing, perspiring, or even walking away from conversations or leaving the room abruptly.

Once safely at home, your partner may feel the need to analyze the situation obsessively, worrying what others thought of her behavior and criticizing herself for not being more talkative, knowledgeable, friendly, and so on, and she may continue to ruminate about the event for an extended period of time afterward. She might even blame you for putting her in the situation in the first place. This dynamic can make both you and your partner wary about future social events.

If your partner has panic disorder, agoraphobia, OCD, or a specific phobia, this can also prevent her from being able to participate in many social events. For example, going to a concert at an arena packed with people probably won't be a pleasant experience, nor would attending a sporting event, going to a movie at a theater, or possibly even eating out. Triggers for anxiety abound in social settings, largely because these situations are beyond your partner's control. As a result, your options for activities as a couple can become severely limited.

Worry Thoughts about Social Situations

People with anxiety about social situations tend to worry about social events beforehand and to ruminate about what they could have done differently or should have done afterward. They tend to overestimate either the likelihood that something bad will happen or the severity of the consequences if the feared outcome actually occurs. Here are some examples of common thoughts related to anxiety in social situations:

- *If I go to this event, I'm going to embarrass myself. Everyone will look at me and know how messed up my life is. I shouldn't even go.*

- *My clothes (hair, job, and so on) aren't good enough for me to attend this function. Everyone will think I'm lazy (ugly, unintelligent, such a slob, and so on).*

- *What if someone asks me a question and I can't get the words out to respond or I say something ridiculous? I'll be so humiliated.*

- *I shouldn't have made that comment. I'm so stupid! I can never show my face there again.*

- *What if the silverware at the restaurant hasn't been washed properly? I'll probably catch some disease and die.*

- *There are going to be thousands of people at the concert. What if I have a panic attack and can't escape?*

Although people who experience anxiety in social settings usually know that their thoughts are distorted, it's still difficult to overcome these thoughts without deliberate effort and practice. And for you, it can be tiring to feel you must constantly reassure your partner that everything is okay.

How Anxiety in Social Settings Can Affect Your Relationship

Having a partner who's prone to anxiety about social situations can have a large impact on your life and your relationship. Positive interactions with others are important for developing and maintaining friendships and other relationships, for connecting to the larger community, and for expanding opportunities, whether professional, such as by networking at a business dinner where partners are invited, or personal, such as when gathering to celebrate the birthday of a friend or family member.

If your partner's anxiety prevents you from socializing with others, the resulting sense of isolation can lead to unhappiness, loneliness, and even depression. In addition, you may feel guilty about missing certain social events and blame your partner. When you have to repeatedly explain why your partner isn't with you or why you need to leave gatherings early, resentment and frustration toward your partner can build up. Other people may ask you outright what's wrong with your partner or stop extending invitations because they expect you'll turn them down.

And because you care about your partner, it can be frustrating for you to hear her disparage herself when you can plainly see that she didn't offend anyone or do anything embarrassing. On the other hand, if others do react negatively to something your partner says or does, it can be challenging to balance supporting your partner with maintaining your relationships with others. You may feel defensive on behalf of your partner and want to protect her or explain her behavior, or you may align with others and feel that your partner needs to learn to manage her anxiety, which can lead to conflicts in your relationship.

Anxiety about social situations can also show up in more subtle ways; for example, your partner may not clearly articulate her anxieties but instead do things like refuse to go to a party or routinely reject your ideas about going out and spending time with others. She may offer vague excuses, such as, "Well, we'll see how I feel that day," or "I'd rather just stay home tonight," leaving you feeling frustrated as you try to figure out why she isn't interested in socializing. Your partner may be ashamed to admit to her anxiety or afraid of disappointing you and therefore resorts to this sort of "wet blanket" mentality to conceal her anxiety.

In chapter 6, you'll find specific strategies to ease your partner's anxiety about social situations and techniques the two of you can practice so that socializing becomes less of a problem for your partner.

EXERCISE: Your Partner's Anxiety in Public

Does your partner become a different person in social situations? Check off all the behaviors you notice your partner engaging in when the two of you are socializing:

_____ *Sitting alone or disappearing for long periods of time*

_____ *Refusing to leave your side*

_____ *Asking to leave early*

_____ *Not contributing to the conversation, even though she is knowledgeable about the topic or attempts have been made to include her*

_____ *Consuming alcohol excessively (relative to her usual amounts)*

_____ *Being irritable or picking a fight with you prior to the event*

Behaviors that occur before or after social situations can also provide clues that your partner has anxiety related to social settings. For example, your partner may frequently turn down invitations or refuse to go to social events, especially at the last minute. Or if she does go, afterward she may engage in a play-by-play analysis of what transpired and her performance during the event. For each behavior you checked off, use your journal to write a description of what happened and how you handled it. Refer back to what you write in response when reading chapters 5 and 6 and consider which of the techniques in those chapters might be most useful for helping your partner cope with social anxiety in the future.

Sexual Intimacy and Anxiety

Sexual problems are frequently cited as a common reason why couples struggle, and if one person in the couple has anxiety, this issue can be even more pronounced. Let's take a quick look at why this is the case. At its most basic level, the function of sex is procreation. Although that may not be what you and your partner are interested in right now, a person's body won't respond appropriately to sexual cues if the environment doesn't feel safe for having offspring. Your partner may need to actively practice relaxation techniques and reframe her anxious thoughts in order to convince her body that she is safe so that sex will be a pleasurable experience.

There may also be specific reasons why your partner feels anxiety around sex, including past trauma, performance concerns, pain during intercourse, feeling unattractive, and religious beliefs that may not align with your expectations for sexual intimacy. Many of these issues are best addressed through professional therapy or, in the case of pain or performance problems, by speaking with a doctor to rule out physical problems.

Behaviors That Indicate Sexual Anxiety

Behaviors that may indicate that your partner is anxious about sexual intimacy include avoiding sex by going to bed early or in a separate room, picking a fight to avoid intimacy, making excuses about why sex isn't a good idea at the time, or insisting on having the lights turned off or having sheets or clothes arranged in a certain way to minimize exposure. Among men, sexual anxiety can make it difficult to achieve or maintain an erection or lead to premature ejaculation or the inability to orgasm. For women, sexual anxiety can cause an inability to orgasm and pain during intercourse and may also contribute to a lack of enjoyment during sex.

Thoughts That Contribute to Sexual Anxiety

Most people experience anxiety around sex at some point in life. But for people who are anxious, the thoughts that accompany sex can be paralyzing and ruin the experience. Here are some of the more common thoughts that occur:

- *If he sees what I look like naked, he won't want to have sex. I'm so fat (hairy, pale, bloated, ugly, and so on).*

- *My anxiety keeps me from being able to maintain an erection. I love her, but I feel like such a loser when I ejaculate too early.*

- *Because I was sexually abused, I'm damaged goods. No one will want to have sex with me.*

- *If I can't bring her to orgasm, it means I'm not a real man. What's wrong with me?*

- *If I don't have sex with him, he'll leave me and find another woman.*

A healthy and satisfying sex life is an essential part of successful partner relationships, and having thoughts like these clearly interferes. Chapters 5 and 6 offer specific techniques that can help your partner reduce anxiety related to sex, which may bring enjoyment back into your bedroom.

How Sexual Anxiety Can Affect Your Relationship

If your partner has anxiety because of a history of sexual trauma, intimacy is likely to be a challenge no matter how close and trusting your relationship. This probably doesn't have anything to do with you; rather, it reflects your partner's need to process the trauma in a safe environment with a trained professional. If your partner is currently working through her trauma in therapy, you may notice a significant decrease in her sexual interest while she's exploring the issue. However, if this decrease in libido continues for very long after processing the trauma with a trained professional, other issues may be interfering with your sexual relationship. In that case, the two of you may want to consider trying couples counseling with a therapist who specializes in sexual issues.

For people with OCD, having sex can be unthinkable. It isn't uncommon for them to have trouble becoming sexually aroused, be afraid of sex, and/or feel outright disgusted by the thought of "contamination" as a result of having sex. These issues can be addressed with appropriate medications and talk therapy.

In addition, if your partner is taking prescription medications, whether to manage anxiety or for another reason, problems with libido may be a side effect. This is extremely common. Your partner may be able to get in the mood for sex but have difficulty reaching orgasm, or may not have any sexual desire at all. If you notice a sudden change in your partner's sexual interest or performance that occurs around the time of changes in medication, it may well be a side effect. Despite how prevalent this issue is, doctors often don't discuss potential sexual side effects when prescribing medication and neglect to ask about changes in sexual functioning during follow-up visits. Unfortunately, it's frequently up to the patient to raise this issue, and yet many people—and especially those with anxiety—are too embarrassed to do so. Encourage your partner to speak up; it won't be the first time the doctor has heard about this problem. The good news is, adjustments to medications can often resolve the issue.

EXERCISE: Your Partner's Anxiety in the Bedroom

Take a few minutes to consider the sexual aspects of your relationship. On a scale of 0 to 10, where 0 means your sex life is nonexistent and 10 means you wouldn't change a thing about your sex life with your partner, how would you rate your current level of satisfaction? Once you assign a rating, create two lists in your journal, one for the positive aspects of your sex life, and the other for negatives. The first might include items such as "We enjoy having sex together"; the other might include items such as "My partner is unwilling to be spontaneous about sex." Once you've made the lists, review them to see which aspects of your sex life appear to be affected by your partner's anxiety.

Emotion Regulation and Anxiety

How many times have you smiled and said, "I'm fine," in response to someone asking how you were doing, when you were actually ready to scream or punch a wall, on the verge of tears, or so exhausted you could practically fall asleep standing up? From a very young age, we're taught to behave in ways deemed socially appropriate despite our true feelings. You can probably remember being told as a kid to pretend you liked a sweater you received for your birthday even though you really wanted a toy. As we get older, these same rules still apply, and they can be the source of considerable anxiety, especially if people feel

Distinguishing between Thoughts and Feelings

Although the terms "thought" and "feeling" are often used interchangeably, it's important for you to distinguish between them when trying to understand your partner's experience. Thoughts are an appraisal of what's going on around us, whereas feelings happen in response to our thoughts. Another way to think about it (although there can be exceptions to this) is that thoughts originate above the neck, while feelings happen throughout the body.

Thoughts and feelings go hand in hand. If your partner thinks she's loved and appreciated, she's more likely to feel happy, content, or satisfied. On the other hand, if your partner thinks she's worthless, incompetent, or stupid, she's likely to feel anxious, depressed, or sad.

The good news is, feelings follow thoughts, and we're capable of changing our thoughts. That's why cognitive behavioral therapy is so effective for anxiety.

as though their emotions or thoughts wouldn't be acceptable to others. If this is the case for your partner, her worries about others finding out "the truth" set up a vicious cycle: having the feeling, worrying about someone discovering that she's having the feeling, suppressing the feeling, the feeling growing more powerful, increasing attempts to suppress the feeling, and so on.

Emotions that are commonly deemed unacceptable include sadness, fear, and anger. Researchers have found that people with anxiety disorders tend to be more sensitive to their emotions (Mennin et al. 2002). Therefore, a situation that would make others feel only slight anger, for example, might provoke strong anger in those with anxiety disorders. In addition, people with anxiety generally don't understand their emotions well, have trouble accepting the emotions they're having, and don't cope or manage their emotions well (Mennin et al. 2002). This means that when your partner gets upset, she may not know what she's feeling or what to do with herself. As a result, she could be prone to taking actions that make things worse rather than better.

How Emotional Sensitivity Fuels Anxiety

People who are emotionally sensitive often react to the world around them as if it's unsafe, similar to how people prone to anxiety and worry tend to have thoughts about potential future danger. While not everyone who is emotionally sensitive experiences excessive anxiety and vice versa, it isn't uncommon to be both anxious and emotionally sensitive.

The tendency to be emotionally sensitive is influenced by both biology and the person's environment. Some people are born with a nervous system that reacts to less intense stimuli that wouldn't affect others. While they can learn to modulate their responses, their sensitivity will always be higher than average.

Environmental factors are particularly influential during childhood. For example, if your partner was taught to view her feelings accurately as she was growing up, perhaps learning from her parents that irritability can be caused by being hungry or tired, then she might have a good understanding of what her feelings mean. On the other hand, if your partner's parents ignored or mislabeled her feelings, perhaps telling her that she wasn't really hungry or tired when, in fact, she was, your partner may never have learned how to appropriately label and respond to what she feels. Knowing that you're having a feeling but being told by your caregivers that you're wrong, or being ignored altogether, can cause anxiety. Unless this mislabeling of emotions is corrected, anxiety related to emotions will continue into adulthood.

Behaviors That Indicate Trouble with Emotion Regulation

It's probably pretty obvious when your partner is struggling with emotion regulation: Things that shouldn't be a big deal are a huge deal, your partner struggles to contain her emotions and is prone to explosions or shutting down, or your partner's reactions to upsetting events take you by surprise because the emotions you would have expected either aren't present at all or are so over-the-top that you wonder if your partner will ever calm down again. Addictive behaviors such as overeating, smoking, or using substances may also indicate that your partner is struggling with emotion regulation. This behavior can arise in response to excessive anxiety but mask the anxiety so that you don't even notice it.

If your partner acts jealous or insecure, this may also indicate emotion regulation problems. Jealousy is a powerful emotion, and if your partner is feeling anxious about the status of your relationship, jealousy can show up in many different forms, including constantly questioning your whereabouts, getting upset if you talk to other people without her knowledge, demanding to be included in everything you do, and frequently asking for reassurance that you love her. When your partner is acting out of jealousy or insecurity, her behavior may become artificial or stilted as she tries to fit into whatever role she thinks you want from her, or she may begin to act in ways you haven't seen before, such as suddenly becoming more interested in having sex or taking an interest in a hobby of yours that she previously didn't care about.

Irritability is another behavior related to struggles with emotion regulation. It often leads to hurtful remarks, disinterest in being social, rudeness, and annoyance. In this case, you may feel as though nothing you do is right in your partner's eyes. In response, you may quickly become annoyed and irritated yourself—which isn't going to help your partner's mood, potentially creating another vicious cycle.

Thoughts That Indicate Trouble with Emotion Regulation

As with many of the other issues discussed in this chapter, thoughts that come with emotion regulation struggles largely revolve around your partner's beliefs about whether she's capable of handling the emotions she's feeling. Here are some examples of thoughts that are typical for people who have difficulties with emotion regulation:

- *It's not okay to be angry. If I show that I'm angry, everyone will think I'm a jerk.*

- *I can't handle this pressure, but if I just have a few drinks, it will be okay.*

- *This is the worst thing that has ever happened to me! I can't deal with this. It's a crisis and no one can help. How am I going to survive this?*

- *I'm not going to talk about how I feel. If I ignore it, it will go away.*

- *If I mess up, my partner will leave me. Nothing I do is right, and I'm afraid he's judging me.*

How Problems with Emotion Regulation Can Affect Your Relationship

If your partner tends to suppress her true emotions, not knowing how she's truly feeling can make it quite difficult to communicate appropriately and find solutions to problems. If you can clearly tell from your partner's behavior that she's upset, but you only get "I'm fine" in response to your questions, it's hard to improve the situation.

On the other hand, your partner may have frequent mood swings. If so, this could indicate a comorbid mood disorder, such as depression or bipolar disorder. Alternatively, she may tend to overreact and display extreme emotion in relatively benign situations. In either of these scenarios, you might become wary of interacting with her because of the potential to make things worse.

Finally, dealing with a jealous or insecure partner can be exhausting. If insecurity is an issue, your partner may frequently seek reassurance, exhausting your energy and patience. With jealousy, you may frequently feel pressured to prove that there's no reason for your partner's feelings. Your partner may also become clingy, causing you to feel suffocated and desperate for time alone, or making you think that nothing you do is ever good enough, so why bother trying?

EXERCISE: Your Partner's Unspoken Emotions

Think of a time when your partner was clearly feeling anxious but wasn't straightforward with you about it. In your journal, answer these questions:

- *What words did she say?*

- *What actions did she take?*

- *What other signs have you noticed that can clue you in to the fact that your partner is feeling anxious but is unable or unwilling to admit it?*

Employment and Anxiety

The ADAA survey of how GAD affects relationships (Russell Research 2004) found that, on average, people with GAD missed fourteen and a half days of work per year due to their anxiety, versus five and a half days missed by those who had neither GAD nor another diagnosable anxiety disorder. Most people with GAD didn't disclose to their employer that anxiety was the reason for some of their absences, probably because more than half of the people surveyed indicated that they were afraid they would lose their job because of the effects of their anxiety on their professional performance. This is yet another example of anxiety creating a vicious cycle: people worry about how their anxiety disorder impacts their professional performance, which creates more anxiety, which probably *does* impact their performance.

Beyond GAD, other types of anxiety can affect employment as well. Those with panic disorder may live in constant fear of having a panic attack in the workplace, among coworkers. They may choose to take a job that never involves presenting at meetings or supervising others. People with OCD may struggle with completing tasks not because they don't want to or don't know how to, but because they feel their work is never good enough. They may obsess over every last detail, missing deadlines and feeling extremely anxious when others evaluate their work. The constraints of specific phobias can impose limits on the opportunities people can pursue. For example, someone with a fear of heights probably won't want an office with a window on the twelfth floor of a high-rise building. Someone who fears flying won't be successful in a job that requires long-distance travel. A person with a fear of bridges probably won't choose to take a job if the commute requires crossing a bridge.

In addition, people with anxiety sometimes find themselves underemployed because of these struggles. To get ahead in a career, people need to have confidence in their skills, be willing to show others what they've accomplished, and make connections that open doors to bigger and better opportunities. All of this can be challenging for people with anxiety, keeping them stuck in jobs that are unsatisfying and don't fulfill their potential. And while your partner may be relieved to have a job that feels safe and predictable, this can also result in depression and feelings of worthlessness if she realizes that others are progressing in their careers and she isn't because of her anxiety.

On the other end of the spectrum, some people with anxiety may work too much or hold themselves to excessively high standards because of their insecurities. Thinking coworkers can't be trusted to do the job right, or fears about being evaluated, falling behind, or not measuring up to their peers are just a few of the reasons why they may spend extra hours at the office or bring work home at night and on the weekends. If your partner does this, obviously it will interfere with her quality of life and limit the time you spend together.

Behaviors That Indicate Anxiety–Related Problems at Work

If your partner has anxiety, navigating relationships with coworkers and supervisors can be especially challenging. She may find many types of work impossible because of fears of being observed, fears about interacting with authority figures, not knowing what to say in social situations, difficulty making eye contact, or problems performing tasks in public. Although people with anxiety typically know that their fears are irrational and desperately want to appear "normal," their traits can make them seem shy, withdrawn, aloof, disinterested, or unfriendly.

If your partner is looking for a job, anxiety makes this tough process even more difficult. Job requirements such as "must be a team player," "need to able to work in a fast-paced environment," and "multitasking skills essential," all of which seem to be listed in almost every job description, can make your partner even more anxious than she already is about applying for positions. This is natural. After all, during an interview she can't disclose that she struggles with anxiety and expect to receive an understanding nod and smile. It will take tremendous effort and courage for your partner to figure out how to land a job where she can be successful. For many anxious people, just putting a résumé in the mail or typing up a cover letter is enough to provoke a fear of being rejected and thoughts that their anxiety will cause them to fail anyway. As for going to an interview, that's stressful for most people, even those who don't tend to be anxious. So much is at stake, especially for people who are unemployed or unhappy in their current job. For your partner, that stress can easily escalate into full-blown panic, ruining her chances for securing the position and setting her up for paralyzing anxiety about future interviews.

Worry Thoughts about Work

"I Submitted the Application, and Therefore, the Job Is Mine!"

Even in today's job market, many people believe that all they have to do is submit a résumé or application and the job will be handed to them. Your partner may be in denial about the additional steps she'll need to take if her application is accepted and the interviewing process begins. Sending in a piece of paper is the easy part. Having to sell herself to strangers who hold her destiny in their hands can provoke a great deal of anxiety. However, she can take many steps ahead of time to help ease her worries, such as talking over common interview questions, thinking about questions she can ask during the interview, deciding what to wear to the interview, and figuring out how much time to allow for getting to the interview.

If your partner has a full-time job, facing anxious thoughts about work is probably an almost daily occurrence that takes a lot of energy and motivation. Depending on the level and type of anxiety your partner is dealing with, she might have anxious thoughts only about specific situations, such as giving a presentation or traveling for business, or she could be struggling with general thoughts about performance and whether she's measuring up. Here are some thoughts that frequently come up for people who have work-related anxiety:

- *What if I mess up this project? I'll be fired and I'll never find another job.*

- *I'm not nearly as smart as the other people in this office. Someone is going to figure that out and tell me I need to leave.*

- *How am I ever going to get this pile of work done? Everyone else seems to be handling their workload just fine. There must be something wrong with me.*

- *If I don't make my sales quota again this month, I'll be demoted and everyone will laugh at me. I'll be so humiliated.*

- *People are just being nice. They don't really mean it when they say I've done a good job. They're probably talking about me behind my back.*

If your partner has thoughts like these running through her head, it can take a tremendous amount of courage to show up at work every day. To get past these thoughts, your partner will need to practice finding evidence against the thoughts and continually remind herself that thoughts are not always reality. (You'll find instructions on how to help your partner with these skills in chapters 5 and 6.) Of course, there are times when your partner's anxious thoughts might be based in reality. For example, if she regularly doesn't make her sales quota, this actually could result in a demotion. If her work-related anxiety is based in reality, it might be worthwhile for her to reexamine her career choices, perhaps with your support or assistance, to see if a different job might be a better fit. (Chapter 4's advice on communication skills will be invaluable if the two of you decide to discuss this issue.)

How Anxiety about Work Can Affect Your Relationship

Work is typically a regular activity for adults, and unlike some anxiety-provoking situations, it's an obligation that isn't easily avoided. The anxiety your partner experiences at work will probably seep into your home life together, as it can be quite difficult to separate the two. Your partner may have a hard time getting motivated to go to work every day and come home anxious at night. Worries about work may affect her sleep and eating habits. Anxiety about her performance at work may spur her to bring work home in an effort to catch up or get ahead, which can cut into your time together as a couple.

In addition, some anxious people find the stress of employment overwhelming and end up being unable to work. The transition to a one-income relationship can affect many aspects of your daily life together. Even if you can provide for your family on your income alone, being the sole breadwinner may not be a role you want. If you're also handling many of the everyday household tasks and family responsibilities on top of a full-time job because of your partner's anxiety, the situation may become unsustainable. If you feel that the situation is unfair, you might also become angry and resentful, which can lead to your partner feeling ashamed or guilty.

EXERCISE: Your Partner's Anxiety at Work

Consider how your partner's work-related anxiety affects your relationship, then read through the following list and check off the statements that apply to you.

_____ Is your partner underemployed or not employed at all?

_____ *Does your partner miss work because of anxiety or anxiety-related symptoms, such as headaches, stomachaches, or fatigue?*

_____ *Do your partner's worries about work-related responsibilities often cut into your time together or diminish your enjoyment in spending time together?*

_____ *Has your partner talked about wanting a different job or wanting to quit working altogether?*

If you answered yes to the last question, what reasons has your partner given for wanting to change jobs? Try to identify the barriers that might stand in her way, such as family finances, lack of opportunities, anxiety about changing jobs, and so on.

For any question you answered yes to, take some time to write in your journal about examples of when this occurred and what happened.

Parenting with an Anxious Partner

Having children provides plenty of opportunities to experience anxiety, even for people not prone to anxiety. For those who are prone to anxiety, worries about parenting can start long before children are even born and then never let up. Most people always feel a degree of concern for their children and therefore worry about their health, safety, and well-being even after their kids are grown, out of the house, and parents themselves. There's no doubt that having children changes a couple's relationship as well. Anxieties about the relationship that neither of you anticipated may surface.

Behaviors That Indicate Anxiety about Parenting

We've all heard about parents who swoop in the instant their child cries or shows any kind of distress, even if the problem is minor. The term "helicopter parents" was coined as one way to describe parents whose anxieties about their kids cause them to hover and attempt to manage every aspect of their children's lives in order to protect them. Beyond this fairly common form of anxiety about parenting, researchers have identified some parenting behaviors specific to people with anxiety disorders (Turner et al. 2003):

- Being highly critical of the child, more so than nonanxious parents

- Showing less affection, smiling less often, and predicting more catastrophes than nonanxious parents

- Being less likely to ask the child's opinion, to accept and respect the child's point of view, and to encourage the child to think independently than nonanxious parents

Parents need not have an anxiety disorder to be anxious about their children. Unfortunately, there are plenty of reasons to worry, and many of them are beyond parents' control. If your partner is prone to excessive worry about these things, she may restrict the activities your children participate in, not allow anyone other than herself and you to care for the children, and "protect" the children from situations she deems dangerous, even if they are age appropriate and safe.

Worry Thoughts about Parenting

Before you and your partner even have children, your partner may experience anxiety regarding infertility. Infertility or worries about it can cause tremendous stress for both partners, and health care providers often don't address this adequately. It can be beneficial for both of you to address current anxieties, such as finances, relationship issues, or past traumas, and take steps to reduce anxiety prior to conception.

During pregnancy, it's common for both partners to have some anxiety: *Is the baby healthy? Am I ready to be a parent? What kind of parent will I be? How will I balance the obligations of being a parent, a partner, an employee, and all of my other roles? How will our lives change?*

When the baby arrives, life changes completely, bringing seemingly unlimited new anxieties: *I'm not ready for this! What does it mean when the baby cries like that? This little being is completely dependent on me. What if I let the baby down? I'm so tired. I'll never be able to manage all of this!*

As the child gets older, the anxieties continue to arise and evolve: *Is he doing well in school? Does she have good social skills? What activities should we put him in so he goes to a good college? Am I too strict? Am I too lenient? What will happen if I let him play football? What if he gets hurt? Should I let her ride in a car with a new driver? What if she gets involved with drugs? What if she gets pregnant? What will others think of me if my kid is "messed up"?*

There are countless ways to worry as a parent. If you and your partner are parents already, you know this. If the two of you are thinking about becoming parents, it's important to consider and address your partner's anxieties so that she'll be in a better position to handle the increased stress that comes with having a child.

How Anxiety Can Affect Parenting and Your Relationship

Anxiety can have a huge influence on parenting. If your partner is overprotective, this can prevent your kids from exploring and experiencing the world in the ways necessary for children to learn. You and your partner may have very different ideas about what's acceptable for your children because of your different perceptions of what is and isn't safe. The advice to let kids be kids may not be okay with your partner if she's afraid of what *might* happen. Remember that anxiety is about perceived dangers, not necessarily what will happen or what's likely to happen. To your partner, the threat of your child being hurt may feel very real, and she may also feel as though she wouldn't be able to manage her emotions if your child were hurt. If something does actually happen, such as the child falling and breaking a bone, your partner may clamp down and refuse to allow your child to do anything even remotely dangerous, even if the chances of injury are slim.

Differences of opinion about parenting can also cause conflict in your relationship. Say your child wants to ride her bike to another friend's house, with friends but without a parent chaperone. You know the route they'll take is safe, but if your child asks your partner, the answer is no. Then your child asks you and you say yes. As a result, not only does your child figure out which of you is more likely to say yes to such requests, but your partner is probably going to be angry with you for not agreeing with her and is also likely to feel increased anxiety because your child is doing something she finds frightening. Being on the same page with your partner regarding parenting is a topic for another book, so just keep this in mind: It's crucial to realize that your partner's anxieties are going to drive the decisions she makes as a parent, and that both of you will have to work extra hard to find workable compromises and deal with the anxiety that arises in the process.

EXERCISE: Parenting When Anxious

If you and your partner have children, take some time to consider the similarities and differences between your parenting styles. Specifically, think about willingness to let your children try new things and whether you allow them the freedom to play and explore independently, then write down some examples of how you handle these situations versus how your partner handles them.

Also consider whether your children tend to come to you or your partner when they want permission to do something that might be dangerous, such as playing sports, going on a ski trip, riding in a car with a newly licensed driver, skateboarding, and so on. Think of some specific examples and write them down.

Finally, consider your reactions versus your partner's reactions when something difficult happens to one of your children, such as getting hurt physically, getting in trouble at school, or doing something embarrassing in public. Again, think of some examples and write them down.

What's Next?

Anxiety can take a heavy toll on a romantic relationship, affecting nearly every area of your life together. However, many other couples face similar challenges, so the two of you aren't alone in this struggle. A variety of techniques and skills can help you reduce and possibly eliminate the difficulties anxiety presents in your relationship. As you read through the rest of this book, you'll learn these techniques and find advice on how to practice them, starting with the next chapter. We'll begin by looking at how *your* thoughts, beliefs, and attitudes about anxiety may be affecting your relationship.

CHAPTER 3

Typical Responses to a Partner's Anxiety

In this chapter, we'll examine some of the thoughts and feelings you may be having about your anxious partner. You may be thinking, *Why look at my thoughts and feelings? I just want to know how to get my partner to stop being so anxious all the time* or *What does it matter how I feel? I'm trying to figure out how to help my partner.* However, identifying and honoring the validity of your thoughts and feelings about your partner's anxiety puts you in a much better position to understand where you need to direct your efforts so that your partner's anxiety won't continue to damage your relationship or perhaps destroy it.

Frustration

Having an anxious partner can be frustrating in many ways. A partner with GAD can frustrate you with constant worries that never seem to be relieved by reassurances that everything is okay. A partner with a specific phobia can be frustrating if the phobia limits what you can do. Perhaps you can't take a vacation you've always dreamed about because your partner is afraid to fly, or you can't live in your dream condo overlooking the city because it means taking an elevator to the twenty-fourth floor. A partner with PTSD can be frustrating if he's constantly vigilant and can't relax enough to enjoy time together even though you've done everything you can think of to make the environment safe and comfortable. A partner with OCD can frustrate you with his insistence that you must wash his clothes immediately, even though it means you'll be late to work, or demands that everything be arranged just so in the kitchen pantry when all you want to do is put the groceries away and get on with the next chore.

A partner who struggles with panic disorder can cause frustration by constantly assessing whether he's likely to have a panic attack or by having one at an inconvenient time. If you have a partner with social phobia, you may feel frustrated by having to make excuses for his behavior or absence, or about the fact that he can't just get over his anxieties, even though he knows the people you're socializing with. Anxious analysis after social encounters can also be frustrating, as he obsesses over little things that were inconsequential to you.

It's completely normal to feel frustrated by a partner's anxiety. Anxiety interrupts life and makes doing everyday things difficult. But if you allow your frustrations to grow into resentment and anger, that won't be helpful or productive. Resentment and anger destroy relationships. Frustration, on the other hand, can be very motivating, so it's important to use that energy in a positive way. This book will provide you with many strategies that can help you channel your frustration productively, particularly chapter 7, which offers lifestyle changes you can implement together to reduce the effects of anxiety on your relationship, and chapter 8, which focuses on taking care of yourself and staying healthy.

EXERCISE: Exploring Frustration

Think of a recent time when your partner's anxiety made you feel frustrated. In your journal, describe the situation:

- *What happened?*

- *What were the circumstances that led up to the point of frustration?*

- *How did you react in the moment?*

- *What did you say and do? How did your partner react to your frustration?*

Anger

At times it may feel as though having a partner with anxiety simply isn't fair. A partner's anxiety can wreak havoc on your life, and it may feel as if your life is diminished and you don't have much control over it because everything revolves around your partner's needs. Your life may become solely about accommodating your partner's anxiety, avoiding places that trigger panic, performing rituals that alleviate his OCD, or not going to social events because he can't handle the perceived scrutiny from others. You may wonder, *How come I'm the one who has to adapt? Why can't he get over it? I'm not the one with the problem!*

You have every right to be angry at the problems your partner's anxiety can cause. But given that you're reading this book, it's likely that you don't want to be angry; rather, you want to figure out how to solve the problem. Like frustration, anger can provide motivation for making positive changes. You can't change your partner overnight, but with time, the techniques and strategies in upcoming chapters can help the two of you alleviate his anxiety and adjust your lifestyle so he's less prone to anxiety.

EXERCISE: Practicing Anger Management

Dealing with angry feelings may seem difficult at times, but you do have choices about how to react when your partner's anxiety makes you angry. Take a look at the following list of techniques that can help you manage your anger. You might want to mark this page or jot down these ideas on a card you can keep in your wallet for handy reference when anger hits. The antianxiety techniques described in chapters 5 and 6 can also be effective in reducing anger.

- **Practice deep breathing,** *inhaling to a slow count to four and exhaling to a slow count to four. Repeat for three minutes.*

- **Repeat a calming word or phrase,** *such as "peace," "calm," or "relax." It may help to focus your gaze on an object or close your eyes while doing this. Repeat the word or phrase until you feel calmer.*

- **Do something that requires you to be quiet and mindful,** *such as stroking a pet, watering plants, stretching gently, or working on a jigsaw puzzle.*

- **Take a time-out,** *giving yourself a few minutes alone. Explain to your partner that you need some time alone and then go somewhere else for fifteen minutes. During that time, you might try some of the other techniques listed here. You might also try journaling about your anger to see if you can come up with a solution to the situation that triggered your anger.*

Because it can be difficult to apply these techniques when you're angry, and possibly even difficult to remember to try using them, it's best to practice them regularly when you aren't angry. This will make them more familiar and easy to implement in challenging situations.

Loneliness

Your partner's anxiety may have turned your relationship into more of a roommate situation, where the two of you live together without sharing your lives. Perhaps there are activities that you'd like to do together that you pursue alone because of your partner's fears. Maybe activities that were once fun to do together have become anxiety-provoking for your partner. It may feel as if your wants and needs don't matter when your ideas and plans are dismissed because of your partner's anxiety. It can feel very lonely to be in a relationship that's dictated by your partner's anxiety.

If your partner's anxiety keeps him stuck in the "safety" of your home and you choose to stay home with him, you'll also miss out on socializing and connecting with others. You can only turn down invitations so many times before people stop extending them. Alternatively, if you do go out on your own, you may miss the companionship of your partner.

You may also feel alone in dealing with your partner's illness. Perhaps it seems as though no one else understands what it's like for you. Family and friends may mean well, but they don't live your life. However, it's still very important to keep those connections so that you aren't isolated, and so that when your partner is functioning well you both have other people to socialize with.

If loneliness is an issue, you may want to consider working with a therapist so you can discuss your feelings and get support. Another possibility is joining a support group for people who have partners with mental illnesses. If there isn't a support group in your community, look for an online group. Knowing that you aren't alone can be a tremendous relief, and hearing about others' experiences can provide validation.

EXERCISE: Combating Loneliness

In your journal, finish this sentence: "I get so lonely when..." Once you've written down what comes to mind, list three to five ways you can reduce your loneliness in that situation. Are there people you can reach out to? Are there activities or hobbies you can engage in with others? Are there social activities you can attend, with or without your partner?

Sadness

You may feel sad that your relationship with your partner isn't what you had envisioned. This is also understandable. Most people have a mental picture of what life will be like when they're in a relationship, and it can be disappointing when those dreams don't come true. Perhaps you're sad about what has happened to your relationship but don't realize it because of other emotions that tend to be stronger and demand more attention, including anger and frustration.

Although we generally associate mourning with death, you have a right to mourn the loss of the relationship you had envisioned, or the loss of the relationship you had before your partner's anxiety took over. Giving yourself time and permission to grieve is important. Just as you need to figure out what your life will be like after someone close to you dies, you need to assess the status of your relationship and decide how to improve the situation and keep moving forward.

Feeling sad can also be a reality check. When you're in a relationship with someone with a mental illness, it's all too easy to become depressed because of your concern, and because of the demands on your time and energy. In addition, since anxiety and depression tend to co-occur, your partner may be depressed. As a result, you may feel sad for him, or his depression may create a subdued, joyless home environment that leaves you feeling down.

If you find that you feel particularly sad, are unable to enjoy things that used to bring you pleasure, and lack energy or motivation, it would be a good idea to talk to a mental health professional to determine whether you're experiencing depression yourself. The self-care suggestions in chapter 8 may also help alleviate your sadness.

EXERCISE: Acknowledging Sadness

In your journal, describe several times when you felt sad as a result of your partner's anxiety. For each situation, write about potential solutions, starting with "Of course I feel sad about [the situation]. Something I can do the next time this happens is..."

Guilt

You may feel that it's wrong to have negative emotions about your partner's anxiety. After all, if you know your partner is struggling, you may think, *What right do I have to feel angry [sad, frustrated, and so on]? He has it much worse than I do.* Actually, you have every right to feel all those emotions and more. Your partner's anxiety has had a negative impact on your life and your plans and dreams.

If you feel guilty for withdrawing from your partner, leaving him out of discussions and decisions that will increase his anxiety, or going to social events while he stays at home alone, understand that this is natural—but not necessary. You can balance that feeling by remembering that you're concerned about your partner and want to help. Reading this book is evidence that you're invested in your partner's wellness and recovery from anxiety. One way to relieve the guilt is to give yourself and your partner time for the suggestions in this book to work.

You don't have to feel guilty because of "negative" emotions about how your partner's anxiety has disrupted your life. Like everyone, you want to be in a healthy relationship with a healthy partner. Talking with family and friends can help you get some perspective on your relationship with your partner. Getting therapy yourself is another strategy, as the therapist can educate you about your partner's illness and offer suggestions about how to manage. Although you probably don't want to tell your partner about all the feelings you're having, keeping those feelings inside isn't healthy either. Talking with others will help you realize that your feelings are normal and acceptable. This should help alleviate your guilt. Chapter 8 is specifically on self-care for you and offers more specific advice on seeking support from others.

EXERCISE: Letting Go of Guilt

Think about a situation when your thoughts and feelings about your partner's anxiety made you feel guilty. What were some of the things you were saying to yourself about your guilt? For example, you may have told yourself, *I shouldn't be feeling this way* or *I'm a bad person for thinking this way about my partner.* Now consider what options you have when you find yourself feeling guilty: Can you change your thoughts? Can you talk to someone who will give you a different perspective? Can you practice acceptance of what is, even though things may not be the way you want? In your journal, make a list of three to five options that are reasonable for you.

Anxiety

It's not uncommon to have anxiety about a partner's anxiety. So many questions come up when you're in a relationship with someone who is anxious: *Will he ever get better? Will the anxiety get worse? Will his anxiety reach the point where he can no longer live a normal life? What if he refuses treatment or the treatment doesn't work? Am I going to develop an anxiety disorder as well, thanks to the ideas he's putting in my head? Will our kids grow up to be anxious too? What if I get sick of dealing with this and want to leave?*

Again, all of these thoughts are completely normal. It's hard to know what the future holds for you and your partner. However, you can reassure yourself by keeping in mind that effective treatments are available and that anxiety is one of the easiest psychiatric illnesses to treat. Treatment does require time and commitment, as well as a lot of support from loved ones, family, and friends—but recovery is possible.

If your own anxiety reaches worrisome levels or you start experiencing symptoms similar to your partner's, you need to seek treatment. It's best to treat anxiety before it becomes severe enough to qualify for a diagnosis of an anxiety disorder. Also, bear in mind that it isn't a good idea to suppress your feelings—including feelings of anxiety. As mentioned in chapter 2, denying feelings or pushing them away only increases their intensity.

EXERCISE: Breaking the Cycle of Anxiety

In your journal, describe a time when your partner's anxieties made you feel anxious as well. What prevented you from feeling or acting calm? What could you have done that would have been more effective for reducing everyone's anxiety in the situation? Make a list of five to seven actions you can take in the future to reduce your own anxiety so that you and your partner avoid feeding off each other's energy. If you can't think of that many strategies at this time, come back to this list later. After you've read chapters 5 and 6, you'll have more techniques to draw from.

Accommodation: How Your Behavior Might Be Making Things Worse

Partners and family members of people with anxiety often try to do whatever they can to relieve the person's anxious feelings. When you live with someone who has anxiety, this can be easier in the short run. As a result, you may find yourself taking on extra responsibilities, avoiding places that make your partner anxious, participating in safety behaviors or rituals with your partner, or handling issues that arise because of your partner's anxiety, such as calling his employer and making up excuses about why he didn't show up for work when the reality is that he's too anxious to go.

Of course, you engage in these accommodations because you care. You may be willing to go to great lengths to ease your partner's anxiety, and this instinct is commendable. Unfortunately, this approach won't improve your partner's mental health in the long run. In fact, it's actually counterproductive. While it can relieve your partner's anxiety in the moment, and you may feel happy about that, ultimately this strategy will make your partner increasingly dependent on you and others who accommodate his anxiety. In essence, you are adjusting and adapting to your partner's fears, which prevents him from learning that he can face and successfully overcome them. This is a key point and can't be overstated, so let me reiterate: By "helping" your partner in this way, you're actually making his anxiety worse, not better.

This can be a tricky concept to understand, so let's take a look at some examples of accommodating an anxious partner and how this backfires in the long run.

> *Jill is a thirty-five-year-old woman who has been married to her husband, Brian, for ten years. When they first met, Jill had some anxiety about driving because of a car accident she was in as a teenager and especially disliked driving alone at night, so Brian did*

all of the driving after dark. Since she didn't have to drive at night very often, Jill's fears were heightened on the occasions when Brian wasn't available to drive her. Jill even missed work some nights when Brian was out of town because of her fears of driving home after dark. Now she completely refuses to drive at night, even though she works as a shift nurse at the local hospital and is currently assigned to the second shift, which ends at 11:30 p.m. Brian, a manager at a local coffee shop, has to be at work at 4:30 a.m. Even though it means he only gets a few hours of sleep, Brian drives Jill to work in the afternoon and stays awake to pick her up and drive her home.

Ben, who is forty-four, has been with his partner, Jim, for six years. Ben dislikes being in crowds and feels uneasy in social situations where he doesn't know anyone. He has a history of panic attacks when around a lot of people. Jim is very outgoing and social. He works as a deejay on the weekends and would love it if Ben would occasionally accompany him to his gigs, but that never happens. In fact, because Ben is so anxious, Jim comes straight home after work and watches television with him when he'd rather be out partying. He does this because he's found that it prevents arguments and reduces the chance of Ben having a panic attack in public. Ben used to be willing to party with Jim every few months or so, but now he's convinced that if he goes out to a club, a panic attack is inevitable. He often tells Jim that he'll meet up with him, but he always ends up canceling at the last minute. When Jim decides to stay out late anyway, he feels guilty about leaving Ben at home alone.

Anna is a fifty-six-year-old woman who has been married to her husband, Ken, for thirty years. Ken has OCD related to whether the oven has been turned off. He insists on checking the oven many *times before he and Anna leave the house and sometimes he demands that they turn around and go home to check the oven again when they're out running errands. Even though she loves to bake, Anna has started avoiding using the oven so she won't exacerbate Ken's anxiety. She used to be able to quell Ken's fears by showing him that she was turning the oven off, but now Ken insists that he needs to check it at least ten times before they can go to bed or leave the house.*

These are just a few examples of the things people do to relieve their partner's anxiety. As you can see, their intentions are good. But to break the cycle of accommodations and escalating anxiety, everyone involved needs to understand that making accommodations strengthens the anxiety in the long run. It sends the anxious person the message that the feared situation truly is dangerous and that he can't handle it. As a result, the situation becomes even more anxiety provoking. Here are some of the accommodation behaviors typical with each type of anxiety disorder.

GAD

- Offering frequent reassurance

- Checking in by phone, email, or text

- Avoiding upsetting conversations

- Hiding information that might trigger anxiety, such as overdue bills or upsetting news stories

OCD

- Washing your hands a certain number of times, as prescribed by your partner

- Doing extra laundry

- Returning home to check whether the oven or iron is off

- Retracing your partner's route to make sure he didn't hit someone with his car

Panic disorder
- Going shopping for your partner

- Taking care of all chores done outside of the house

- Accompanying your partner anytime he leaves the house

- Giving your partner frequent reassurances about safety

- Avoiding places where your partner fears having a panic attack

PTSD
- Avoiding places where the traumatic event took place

- Avoiding discussing the traumatic event and telling others to not talk about it either

- Walking on eggshells to avoid upsetting your partner

Social phobia or social anxiety disorder
- Declining invitations

- Making excuses about why your partner can't go to work or attend a party

- Answering questions on your partner's behalf in social situations

Specific phobia

- Driving long distances when flying would be more convenient

- Checking for the presence of whatever your partner fears (dogs, insects, snakes, and so on) before your partner enters an area

- Monitoring the weather forecast and making sure your partner knows when a storm is coming so he can "protect" himself

- Telling your partner to close his eyes when you drive over a bridge

Accommodations as Demotivators for Treatment

Another downside of making accommodations for your partner's anxiety is that it sends the message that there's no need to pursue treatment. After all, your partner will expect that you'll just step in and make everything okay. Therapy for anxiety takes a lot of hard work, determination, and courage. If your partner knows that you'll make changes to relieve his distress, why should he make any efforts to change?

This is especially important when the anxiety stems from trauma or fears that your partner must face in order to work through his anxieties. For example, if your partner is afraid to drive, it's far easier for him to have you drive him everywhere than to talk to a therapist about the real reasons why he's afraid to drive, which may bring up painful memories. Although you may want to alleviate your partner's discomfort due to anxiety, that discomfort is exactly what will provide motivation to engage in the challenging work of treatment.

Accommodations as Affection

Sometimes accommodation behaviors become the main way a supportive partner shows affection and love for the anxious partner. It can become a comfortable role to be the hero, stepping in to save your partner from fearful situations. This can range from little things, like being the designated insect killer or buying extra cleaning products to accommodate cleaning rituals, to major accommodations, such as offering to drive two thousand miles to a family reunion instead of flying or taking a job that will allow you to come home at a moment's notice if your partner is having a panic attack, even though you aren't really interested in the job.

While you might think these choices are simply a way of showing that you love and care about your partner, as you now know, they actually make things worse. Your partner will become increasingly dependent on you to step in and do whatever is necessary to prevent or relieve his anxiety. And when you aren't willing or able to do so, your partner may feel abandoned and angry—not to mention extremely anxious!

Validation Isn't the Same as Agreement or Accommodation

You can validate your partner's discomfort without agreeing that his anxiety is warranted or making accommodations. For example, you can say, "I hear you that you're nervous about going to the party" (validation). Try stopping right there without going on to say, "And you may be right that you'll make a fool of yourself"(agreement, even if you don't believe it to be true), or "Why don't you stay home tonight?" (accommodation). I'll cover validation in depth in the next chapter and explain its benefits. For now, just understand that when I recommend not accommodating your partner's anxieties, I'm not asking you to invalidate them. Those thoughts and feelings are real to your partner, even if they aren't justified.

Accommodations as an Occasional Strategy

It would be great if stopping accommodations were as easy as flipping a light switch, but these behaviors can be ingrained and hard to let go of. Plus, there will probably be some times and situations where accommodating your partner's anxiety might make sense. For instance, if he has truly been making an effort to change but for some reason can't do something that needs to be done today because it provokes anxiety, perhaps letting him off the hook would be validating and provide some positive reinforcement for the times when he has been successful in facing his fears. No one is perfect, and everyone needs a break every once in a while. Using accommodations judiciously can help strengthen your relationship and your partner's commitment to changing.

EXERCISE: Identifying Your Accommodations

In your journal, or perhaps on a separate piece of paper, make a list of things you've been doing.in an effort to alleviate your partner's anxiety. Keep this list handy as you continue reading the book to serve as a reminder of what isn't helpful, and add to it as you notice other accommodation behaviors. In upcoming chapters, I'll provide a variety of techniques you can use to help your partner overcome his anxiety, rather than perpetuating the problem.

Managing Your Resources

The writing exercises you did in this chapter probably gave you new insights into how your partner's anxiety affects you and may have inspired thoughts about what you'd like to do to improve your relationship. But before you start drafting the "perfect" solution, step back for a moment and consider how you and your partner got to where you are today. These issues didn't develop overnight, and if there were an easy fix, you and your partner probably would have found it by now.

Deciding how to approach your partner's anxiety and the difficulties it causes isn't like fixing a leaky toilet, where you can go to a hardware store, find the part you need, install it, and be done. Addressing anxiety and the relationship issues it can cause is more like long-term maintenance, similar to managing your finances: something you always need to be aware of, and something that can change quickly. If you and your partner both had full-time jobs and then one of you was laid off, your financial situation would change rapidly and dramatically. Together, you would adjust to the change in cash flow, and then, when things inevitably changed again in the future, you'd adjust again. Dealing with your partner's anxiety is similar. Ideally, you'd be able to work together to find permanent solutions to the worries, perhaps through targeted treatment and the lifestyle changes discussed in chapter 7. However, the more realistic scenario is that your partner's anxiety will be a factor in your relationship at least some of the time. Therefore, it's best to focus on anxiety management, rather than hoping for a hard-and-fast solution.

What's Next?

It's natural to have negative feelings if your partner has an illness, no matter what kind of illness it is. Rather than feeling guilty about your feelings, use them as motivation to make changes. The remainder of the book will give you plenty of specific strategies to use, starting with communication skills in the next chapter, so you can talk with your partner about your concerns and your ideas about how you can work together effectively.

CHAPTER 4

Communication Strategies That Can Help with Anxiety

Hearing the words, "Honey, we need to talk" tends to raise our blood pressure by a few points. The anxiety of not knowing what's coming next causes most people to start thinking, *Uh-oh. What did I do wrong?* Because your partner is already prone to anxiety, telling her, "We need to talk," is likely to set off a more extreme reaction than a non-anxious person would experience. However, that doesn't mean serious discussions are completely off the table. That would just be another accommodation to prevent your partner from feeling anxious, and as you now know, that isn't in your partner's best interests. What it does mean is that you'll both benefit from using various communication skills to ensure that your discussions are effective.

This chapter offers numerous useful techniques that can make difficult discussions easier and more productive. It will also help you identify behaviors that signal that your partner is feeling anxious and provide some pointers on how to respond appropriately.

Understanding Good Communication

You would think good communication skills would be taught in kindergarten. After all, the ability to articulate our needs to get what we want while remaining sensitive to the needs of others is one of the most important skills in life. Unfortunately, most of us have to learn these skills on our own—often through observation—and our role models may not have had the greatest communication skills themselves. The reality is, most people aren't really good at both speaking and listening, two essential components of effective communication. On the upside, it's never too late to learn or improve these skills.

In addition to making use of good speaking and listening skills, good communication between partners—anxious or not—has several key qualities:

- Both partners are able to express their feelings openly and directly, without fear of reprisal or attack from the other.

- Both partners can listen nondefensively when the other person talks.

- There is mutual respect even when dealing with disagreement, anger, or frustration.

Poor communication is the opposite: Rather than being open, clear, and direct, it's characterized by shutting down or acting out frustrations aggressively (for example, yelling or making threats) or passive-aggressively (for example, saying, "Whatever... I don't care," or vaguely suggesting that something bad will happen if the other person doesn't comply with a request). It involves interrupting, arguing defensively, or insisting that the other person is wrong, rather than listening to the other person's perspective. It can also show up as blaming or looking for ways to put the other person down instead of conveying love and respect, accepting responsibility, and working together to solve the problem.

Why Good Communication Is Especially Important When One Partner Has Anxiety

While everyone can benefit from good communication skills, it's especially important to use them with people who are prone to anxiety. This helps keep the conversation focused on the subject at hand, rather than getting derailed if the person's anxiety is triggered by the dialogue. In order to have productive and mutually supportive conversations with your partner, you'll need to be especially skilled at communicating well.

The major focus of this chapter is tools for both speaking and listening—tools you can pull out and use when appropriate. Just as with a real toolbox, not every tool can solve every problem, and different tools are appropriate for specific contexts. You *could* use a screwdriver to make holes in a wall, but a drill would be more efficient and effective. Having a variety of tools to choose from, depending on the situation, can make the difference between a positive conversation that ends with both people feeling loved, cared for, and heard and a discussion that becomes a painful argument or fight.

Speaking Tools

The following seven speaking tools are essential for effective communication. As with using any new tool, it will take time and practice to master these techniques. If a tool doesn't work in one conversation, that doesn't mean it won't be appropriate or helpful another time. Keep working at it! Also be sure to observe your partner carefully during conversations. She may respond to certain tools better than others. If you know this, you can focus on using those more often.

Tool 1: Show Empathy

Sometimes people confuse empathy with sympathy. Being empathetic means conveying that you have some sense of your partner's experience and being genuine in your concern. Sympathy means feeling sorry for your partner, which won't be helpful in countering your partner's anxiety. To appropriately convey empathy, put yourself in your partner's shoes and try to see the world through her eyes. Being empathetic means communicating that you understand that the situation is challenging, even if you don't agree with her perspective or response. Here are some examples of anxiety-related statements and how you might respond to them empathically.

Anxious partner: *I'm worried that I won't be able to handle all the new job responsibilities my boss is heaping on me.*

Empathetic response: *It must be scary to feel like your job is too much to handle.*

Empathetic response: *I can hear that you're really concerned about doing a good job.*

Anxious partner: *I hate going to parties. It feels like everyone is always looking at me.*

Empathetic response: *It sounds like going to parties is really uncomfortable for you. I sometimes feel that way too.*

Empathetic response: *I understand that you don't enjoy parties and don't like being the center of attention.*

Anxious partner: *I can't go to the family reunion this year. I know I'll have a panic attack if I have to get on a plane.*

Empathetic response: *You're really worried about having to fly.*

Empathetic response: *It seems like thinking about getting on a plane is overwhelming for you.*

Anxious partner: *If the towels aren't hung the way I want in the bathroom, I can't leave for work until they're fixed.*

Empathetic response: *You sound really concerned about this.*

Empathetic response: *It's upsetting for you when things aren't done just right.*

Using empathic statements conveys that you understand your partner without trying to solve the problem. Although you may think that solving the problem is helpful, remember that this is another form of accommodation. Your partner is capable of finding her own solution or can ask you for help if it's needed. Just one caution: When using empathy it can be easy to cross the line into being condescending, especially if you don't agree with your partner's perspective. Be careful about your tone of voice. You may find it helpful to practice making empathic statements during everyday conversations with a variety of people to give you some experience in using this skill.

Tool 2: Inquire about Your Partner

Conversations should be a two-way street. It's important to know what your partner is thinking and feeling as you talk. The purpose of inquiry is to make sure your partner is receiving your message accurately, which can clear up any misunderstandings in the moment, rather than allowing them to linger—possibly long after the conversation is over. Inquiry also allows you to gain clarity about your partner's experience and ensures that she feels she has a say in the conversation. It's especially useful after you've made a point. Here are some examples of how you might utilize inquiry (note that inquiry need not be phrased as a question):

- *Am I making sense?*

- *Can you tell me what you're thinking right now?*

- *Tell me what your thoughts are about this.*

- *I'd like to know what you think about what I just said.*

Tool 3: Use "I" Statements

Using "I" statements is an effective way to convey how you feel to your partner. Starting sentences with "I" instead of "you" avoids placing blame on your partner and opens the door to collaborating on a solution. Take a look at the following examples to see how much difference this small change can make. Which type of statements do you think your partner would be more responsive to?

"You" statement: *You're going to kill someone with your fear of driving over bridges!*

"I" statement: *I get really nervous about what happens to you when you have to drive over a bridge.*

"You" statement: *You worry too much about what other people think of you.*

"I" statement: *I'm concerned that your fears about what others think of you are holding you back at work.*

"You" statement: *Your excessive hand washing is out of control!*

"I" statement: *I'm worried that your need to wash your hands all the time is interfering with your life.*

"You" statement: *Your worry about everything—money, the kids, our house, the weather—is driving me crazy!*

"I" statement: *I feel anxious when you bring up your anxieties every time we talk. Could we maybe decide on a time each day to discuss your concerns and agree to talk about other things the rest of the time?*

"You" statement: *You're making everyone uncomfortable with your need to constantly pace the room.*

"I" statement: *I get concerned when I see you struggling to relax and enjoy being with us.*

Tool 4: Give Positive Feedback

People like to hear that they're loved and appreciated. However, if you're feeling upset because of something your partner has done or said, it can be hard to remember why you love her in the first place. During difficult conversations about the relationship, bear in mind that your partner probably feels very vulnerable, and that hearing something positive can go a long way toward reassuring her. What do you love about your partner? Think about special qualities that you admire in her and find a way to let her know, despite whatever is going on in the moment, that you truly love and care about her. Find something genuinely positive to say about your partner during the conversation. Again, the key is being genuine; your partner will see right through you if you're lying or being condescending. Here are a few examples of how you might offer positive feedback:

- *I really appreciate how hard you've been trying.*

- *I know this can't be easy, and I have so much respect for what you've accomplished.*

- *I've been asking you to do some hard things. I'm really grateful to you for trying.*

- *You are simply amazing—I'm so lucky to have you as my partner!*

Tool 5: Be Direct

In the course of difficult conversations, it can be easy to get side-tracked into irrelevant details or to edge around the real topic at hand. Although taking an indirect approach may seem like a softer way to get into a difficult topic, it actually prolongs the misery of anticipation for both you and your partner. Get to the point, and get to it quickly—but don't take this as license to attack your partner with the first words out of your mouth. Be respectful and lead into the topic succinctly by saying something like "I appreciate your taking the time to talk with me. I've been thinking about this for a while, and we need to discuss…"

Tool 6: Keep It Short

Your partner might experience physiological responses related to anxiety, such as shortness of breath and sweating, during difficult conversations. If so, her ability to process lengthy statements from you will be limited. While you don't need to talk to your partner like a child, it will be helpful if you keep your sentences brief and to the point. If you talk for more than thirty seconds without stopping, you're going on too long.

Tool 7: Make Specific Requests

It isn't enough to simply communicate, "Your anxiety is driving me crazy. Stop it!" After all, if that were effective, you and your partner probably wouldn't have a problem. If you truly want to improve the situation, you need to help your partner understand exactly what needs to change. Here are a few examples of how to make specific requests.

General statement: *Don't call me at work so much.*

Specific statement: *It would be helpful if you would try some of the techniques you've learned for calming yourself down before calling me at the office.*

General statement: *You're making me late again!*

Specific statement: *I've been late to work too many times because of your habit of checking the door locks. We need to figure out a way to get me there on time.*

General statement: *Going to parties with you is awkward.*

Specific statement: *When you're feeling uncomfortable at a party, it would help me a lot if you could give me a signal so we can make an exit without seeming rude.*

General statement: *I'm uncomfortable when you act anxious.*

Specific statement: *I'm never sure how you want me to respond when you tell me you don't want to go to work because you're too anxious. How can I best help you when that happens?*

Listening Tools

Remember, good communication involves two sets of skills: speaking skills and listening skills. Listening skills will help you understand your partner's perspective and ensure that you're both on the same page during important conversations. Clearly, listening well is critical to good communication; in fact, it's often more important than speaking well. Finding a good balance between speaking and listening can be hard, but it's worth the effort. Your partner will appreciate it whenever you use any of the six tools of listening described below.

Tool 1: Eliminate Distractions

How many times have you been interrupted by a phone call, pets, or children when trying to have an important conversation with your partner? You both need and deserve each other's full attention when discussing your relationship, so do whatever you can to prevent distractions. Here are a few examples of how you might set the stage for this:

- *I'm going to turn off the television while we talk, because we both need to listen carefully to what is said.*

- *Let's turn off our phones while we have this discussion so we're not distracted.*

- *Why don't we talk when the kids are at their friend's house and we know we'll have some uninterrupted time?*

- *I'd appreciate it if you would take a break from playing that game so we can discuss this.*

Tool 2: Use and Observe Body Language

A great deal of communication occurs via body language. Your partner's body language can offer many clues about her experience of anxiety. This may show up as behaviors or physiological signs, and it can also make an appearance as verbal behaviors that go beyond the meaning of the words she says (such as with sarcasm). Understanding these signs can give you a lot of information about what's happening with your partner—even if she's verbally saying, "Everything is fine" or "No, I'm not worried about this." Here are some of the common ways that anxiety shows up in body language.

Behaviors
- Fidgeting

- Not making eye contact

- Darting eyes

- Nail biting

- Hair twirling

- Having a rigid or tense facial expression

- Picking at clothes or something on the body

- Having crossed arms

- Hand twisting

- Changing body positions frequently

- Chewing on pens, nails, or lips

- Trembling

- Tapping the fingers or feet

- Whistling

- Jingling the contents of pockets

Physiological signs

- Shallow, rapid breathing

- Flushing

- Paleness

- Wide eyes

- Crying

- Clearing the throat

- Sighing

- Sweating

Verbal cues

- Having an irritated tone of voice

- Being sarcastic

- Making smart-alecky comments

- Changing the topic

- Speaking more softly or loudly than usual

- Having a quivering voice

- Speaking quickly

When you notice these signs in your partner, you can use your speaking tools of empathy and inquiry to show that you understand what your partner is feeling and find out how you can help your partner feel less anxious.

You can also facilitate conversations by using body language to show your partner that you're relaxed and receptive. Adopt an open posture, with your arms uncrossed. Lean forward slightly, make good eye contact, and nod your head to indicate that you're listening. Keep your hands away from your face and hair (which may indicate you are feeling anxious yourself) and smile (for real—not a fake, plastered-on smile).

Tool 3: Avoid Interrupting

Not interrupting is a challenge for a lot of people. Do your best to keep your mouth shut and wait your turn to speak. The only exception is if you need clarification, and even then, keep it brief; for example, "Sorry to interrupt, but I didn't catch that last part. Can you please repeat it?" or "Wait, I think I missed something. Can you say that again?"

Tool 4: Use Reflective Listening

Because reflective listening involves speaking it may not seem like a listening skill. However, the point here is to echo back what your partner said to indicate that you were listening and be sure you understand. Try not to sound like a parrot, repeating what your partner said word for word; that can be annoying and counterproductive. Like empathy, it takes practice to get right, and you can use it in any conversation to get more comfortable with it.

Anxious partner: *I really don't want to drive to the store to get groceries when it's dark outside.*

What not to say: *Driving at night is no big deal. I know you can handle it.*

Reflective statement: *I remember that you asked me to drive you to the store the other night too, but you didn't say why. Is this something we need to figure out?*

Anxious partner: *I hate going to office parties with you. None of the other wives like me.*

What not to say: *You're the most beautiful woman there. Everyone loves you!*

Reflective statement: *I want to make sure I understand what you've said. You feel uncomfortable going to office functions with me because you feel like the other women don't like you.*

Anxious partner: *I don't like it when I can't reach you on your cell phone. I get nervous that something has happened to you.*

What not to say: *You need to get over it. I'll call you back when I can.*

Reflective statement: *You get concerned if I don't answer my phone when you call.*

Anxious partner: *It's hard for me to sleep in the same bed as you. I have nightmares about what happened, and I don't want to wake you up.*

What not to say: *I sleep like a rock. You won't wake me up.*

Reflective statement: *So you're worried that if we sleep in the same bed, your nightmares will wake me up too?*

Tool 5: Clarify Implied Statements

Your partner may be too anxious to come right out and say what she means. There could be a lot of reasons for this: she may be worried about your response, concerned about hurting your feelings or making you angry, or embarrassed, to name a few. As a result, she may be indirect in her speech. This tool is the listening counterpart to the speaking tool of making specific requests. Clarifying what your partner means is crucial to communicating effectively and avoiding misunderstandings. Here are some examples of implied statements and how you might respond to them.

Anxious partner: *You know what I mean.* (Or *You know what I'm trying to say.*)

Clarifying response: *Actually, I need some help figuring out what you mean.*

Anxious partner: *You should know how I feel about that.*

Clarifying response: *I'm actually a little unsure how you feel about that. Can you be more specific?*

Anxious partner: *It wasn't that bad.*

Clarifying response: *What do you mean by 'It wasn't that bad'?*

Anxious partner: *It will be fine. Don't worry about it.*

Clarifying response: *I am worried about things, and I want to help you. Can you help me understand your perspective better?*

Tool 6: Acknowledge Your Partner's Point of View

As with reflective listening, acknowledging your partner's point of view involves speaking, but the purpose is to show that you've been listening. In challenging conversations, it can be difficult to see both sides of the story, especially if the issue has been building over time and you're having strong feelings about what's going on. Acknowledging that you've heard what your partner said and validating her words will go a long way toward achieving effective communication. Here are a few examples of how to use this skill:

- *Thanks for taking the time to explain [describe the situation]. Now I have a much better idea what's happening for you.*

- *I can understand why [describe the situation] makes you anxious! How can we work together to make it better?*

- *Before you told me about [describe the situation], I had no idea it was causing you such anxiety. Now I can see things from your perspective.*

Communication Traps to Avoid

There are as many ways to derail a conversation as there are skills to enhance communication. Often, it's best to avoid having sensitive discussions altogether in certain situations. Here are some examples:

- In public places

- In the company of friends, family members, or coworkers

- The minute your partner gets home from work

- First thing in the morning, late at night, or in the middle of the night

- When either of you is already upset

- When outside distractions, such as kids, television, or phone calls, make it impossible to talk uninterrupted

- Right before, during, or after sex

- Just as one of you is going out the door

If Your Partner Gets Upset

A major reason to use the tools of speaking and listening in this chapter is to prevent the conversation from triggering your partner's anxiety. However, this may not always be possible. Conversations go awry for everyone. Having a tough conversation with an anxious partner only ups the ante. If a conversation doesn't go well, there could be myriad reasons why, and it may be that none of them have anything to do with you or your communication skills. The timing could have been off. Your partner may have had a bad day at the office or with the kids. Maybe there were interruptions, or maybe your partner was just tired and not in a good frame of mind for a discussion.

Here are a few tips on how to respond if your partner gets upset, with examples of each. Read through this list closely and keep these techniques in mind so you can use them when needed:

- **Don't fight back.**
  - *I don't want to argue with you about this, but I do want to hear what you have to say.*
  - *Let's not fight about who's right or wrong; let's talk this out.*

- **Maintain self-control.**
  - *I'm going to stay calm during this discussion because I think and communicate better that way.*
  - *I'm not going to lose my temper and say something I'll regret later.*
  - *Let's both take a minute to calm down, and then we can resume the conversation.*

- **Listen, empathize, and acknowledge your partner's feelings.**
  - *I absolutely hear you that you thought my behavior was insensitive, and now that you've explained your side of things, I understand why.*
  - *If I had been that anxious in that situation, I probably would have acted the same way.*
  - *Now that I know how terrified you were by that, I get why you said what you did.*

Find a compromise.
  - *So, now that we both know how we feel, let's think about how we can do things better next time.*
  - *When you aren't happy, I'm not happy, so how about we work together to figure out a solution?*

If these techniques don't work and, upon reflection, you feel you did the best you could, then leave it at that. Regroup and try to have the discussion later. If you can identify what went wrong, then commit to practicing the communication tools that might help the conversation go better next time. Give your partner time and space to calm down, and negotiate another time to continue the discussion.

Staying Optimistic

As long as you believe that you and your partner can work through the anxiety issues that have caused difficulty in your relationship, all of the tips and tools in this chapter will be helpful. If, on the other hand, you think that things won't get better unless your partner changes, they are much less likely to help. It's true that our attitudes and beliefs can create a self-fulfilling prophecy, so keep things positive. Even if the tools you try aren't always effective, don't give up all hope. Just because one discussion doesn't go as planned, don't stop trying, because then you're truly unlikely to ever see any results.

These techniques take time and practice to master. You might be lucky and use them successfully the first time, but that's rare. Even trained mental health professionals don't get it right every time. What's most important is that you keep trying, and that both you and your partner are committed to making changes to improve the relationship. Look at it this way: if you keep doing what you've always done, you're likely to remain stuck in the same rut.

What's Next?

This chapter offered a variety of tools for effective communication. These skills will strengthen any relationship, but they are especially important when one partner has anxiety, allowing both of you to keep your focus on the topic at hand rather than getting swept up in your partner's anxious thoughts. These skills will also allow you to better understand your partner's situation, opening the door to more effective responses when anxiety strikes—the topic of the next two chapters. Chapter 5 provides techniques that promote relaxation and a sense of calm; practicing them regularly will be helpful for both of you. It will also enhance your ability to implement the strategies you'll learn in chapter 6, which are specific to different types of anxiety.

CHAPTER 5

Techniques for Reducing Anxiety and Promoting Relaxation

In this chapter, I provide exercises that are appropriate for any type of anxiety and that can help anyone, anxious or not, relax and reduce stress. Some of these techniques can be used to relieve anxiety in the moment, whereas others are recommended as daily practices to reduce anxiety overall. In chapter 6, I'll address how to respond to specific types of anxiety: acute, chronic, and as manifested in the six diagnosed anxiety disorders.

Hopefully, you and your partner will try all of the techniques in this chapter. That will give you more strategies to choose from when anxiety strikes, and will also allow you to learn what's most effective for reducing your partner's anxiety.

I highly recommend that you practice all of these techniques yourself. This will allow you to provide more effective support for your partner in using them. Plus, you're undoubtedly familiar with how stressful it can be to live with a person who struggles with anxiety. There's a very good chance that you can also benefit from these techniques. Finally, as you'll learn in chapter 6, one key to responding effectively to your partner's anxiety in the moment is to remain calm yourself. Practicing the techniques in this chapter can help you do that. For these reasons, when giving instructions for the exercises in this chapter, I generally use the word "you" to indicate the person doing the exercise, which may be you, your partner, or, hopefully, both of you.

Distraction with Pleasurable Activities

It probably won't come as a surprise that distraction with pleasurable activities is a popular relaxation technique among the many clients I've worked with. While the strategy is simple, in difficult times it can be hard to remember the activities that you might find pleasurable. I recommend making one list of activities that you and your partner can engage in together when your partner needs a distraction, and another list of activities your partner can do on his own. Here are some examples to get you going:

- Watching a funny movie or television show

- Going for a walk, a run, or a bike ride

- Cleaning house or washing the car

- Doing a hobby, such as painting, drawing, sewing, quilting, or playing a musical instrument

- Gardening or doing other outdoors work

- Getting a massage

- Cooking a new recipe

- Working on a puzzle

- Listening to music that lifts your mood

- Reading

- Playing a game

Practicing Mindfulness Together

Mindfulness practice has roots in Buddhist philosophy, but you and your partner need not subscribe to any kind of doctrine or philosophy to incorporate mindfulness into your life. In essence, mindfulness, which is a form of meditation, involves bringing awareness to the present moment and simply noticing what's happening without judging, criticizing, or trying to change your internal experience.

Since much of what causes anxiety in your partner is the inability to control his thoughts, achieving a place of mindfulness can provide relief. Let's look at how that works: In mindfulness practice, the focus is on the present moment, whereas when your partner feels anxious, his thoughts are likely to be about what's going to happen in the future. As he consciously brings awareness to what's happening in the moment, his anxious thoughts are less likely to intrude. When they do creep in, the solution is simply to refocus attention on the present.

Another benefit of mindfulness is the realization that thoughts are transient. People who are anxious often get caught in a loop in which the same worries repeat themselves over and over again. Practicing mindfulness stops the loop, and the thoughts often become less potent or even disappear as a result.

In this section I'll describe mindful breathing and a mindful body scan. These are just two of the many mindfulness techniques you might practice. If you find mindfulness helpful and would like to try other techniques, you'll find many good sources of information both online and in print (see Resources). You may be able to find a local class on mindfulness, which would be an excellent way to get acquainted with a variety of techniques and begin a regular practice.

Mindful Breathing

One of the most universal and basic mindfulness techniques is counting breaths. Everyone breathes and we do it all the time, so this focus for mindfulness is portable and convenient, requiring nothing more than tuning in to the breath. This technique is an effective way to learn to focus on the present moment and develop concentration. You may want to start with five minutes and work your way up to twenty to thirty minutes of uninterrupted mindful breathing. Decide how long you'll practice, then consider setting a timer or alarm so you won't be distracted by checking the time.

1. Sit in a comfortable, upright position with your feet flat on the floor and your hands resting on your lap, palms facing up or down. You can either close your eyes or keep them open, gazing softly at an object several feet away.

2. Focus on your breathing and try to feel whether it's coming from your chest or your abdomen. Try to soften and relax the area where you feel your breath. Pay attention to the sensation of your breath moving in and out of your body.

3. Allow your breath to move naturally. Don't try to control its pace or breathe more deeply. Your only job in this moment is to focus on your breath.

4. When your mind wanders (and it will—many, many times), just notice that this has happened and return your attention to your breath. Try not to make judgments about the fact that

your mind wandered, how many times it has wandered, or what it has wandered to. A wandering mind is to be expected. Simply keep bringing your focus back to your breath, again and again.

5. When your time is complete, slowly open your eyes if they were closed and stretch your body. Notice any thoughts or feelings you may be having about your mindfulness practice. Recognize that some days will be more enjoyable than others.

Body Scan

While most people hold tension in various parts of the body, this is even more pronounced in people with anxiety. Performing a mindful body scan can help you reconnect with your body and relax by focusing attention on specific parts of the body in sequence and releasing any tension you notice. Allow yourself at least thirty minutes to practice this technique.

The body scan is best done while lying down. Before beginning the practice, spend two to three minutes lying comfortably on your back and focusing on breathing in and out from your abdomen. This will help you to turn your thoughts away from the stressors of the day and inward to your body sensations. It also gives you time to make sure you're in a comfortable position. Once you feel that you're present and ready for the exercise, you can begin.

1. Focus on the toes of your left foot. For about thirty seconds, simply notice whatever sensations are happening only in that part of your body. Don't evaluate them, labeling them as "good," "bad," "uncomfortable," and so on. Simply notice them for what they are. Take a breath and imagine the breath is in the toes of your left foot. Exhale and imagine your breath,

and any tension, being released through the toes. Repeat twice more, noticing the physical sensations in the toes of your left foot, and inhaling, exhaling, and releasing tension through the toes.

2. Turn your focus to your entire left foot. Again, notice the sensations in your left foot for about thirty seconds without making judgments. Breathe in and out of your left foot three times, releasing any tension as you exhale.

3. Focus on your left lower leg in the same way: noticing sensations, then inhaling and exhaling through your left lower leg three times and releasing any tension as you exhale.

4. Focus on your left thigh in the same way: noticing sensations, then inhaling and exhaling through your left thigh three times and releasing any tension as you exhale.

5. Turn your focus to the toes of your right foot, noticing sensations, then inhaling and exhaling through the toes of your right foot three times and releasing any tension as you exhale.

6. Work your way up through your right foot, lower leg, and thigh in the same way: noticing sensations, then inhaling and exhaling through each part of the leg three times and releasing any tension as you exhale.

7. Proceed through your torso in the same way: buttocks, lower back, abdomen, ribs, chest, and upper back. For each area, focus your attention in the same way: noticing sensations, then inhaling and exhaling through that area of the body three times and releasing any tension as you exhale.

8. Turn your focus to the fingers of your left hand, noticing sensations, then inhaling and exhaling three times and releasing any tension as you exhale.

9. Focus on your left hand in the same way: noticing sensations, then inhaling and exhaling through your left hand three times and releasing any tension as you exhale.

10. Focus on your left lower arm in the same way: noticing sensations, then inhaling and exhaling through your left lower arm three times and releasing any tension as you exhale.

11. Focus on your left upper arm in the same way: noticing sensations, then inhaling and exhaling through your left upper arm three times and releasing any tension as you exhale.

12. Focus on your left shoulder in the same way: noticing sensations, then inhaling and exhaling through your left shoulder three times and releasing any tension as you exhale.

13. Turn your focus to the fingers of your right hand, noticing sensations, then inhaling and exhaling through the fingers of your right hand three times and releasing any tension as you exhale.

14. Work your way up through your right hand, lower arm, upper arm, and shoulder in the same way: noticing sensations, then inhaling and exhaling through each part of the arm three times and releasing any tension as you exhale.

15. Turn your focus to your neck, noticing sensations, then inhaling and exhaling through your neck and releasing any tension as you exhale.

16. Turn your focus to your face—jaw, mouth, eyes, forehead—all of your face, noticing sensations, then inhaling and exhaling through your facial muscles and releasing any tension as you exhale.

17. Turn your focus to the back and top of your head, noticing sensations, then inhaling and exhaling through the back and top of your head and releasing any tension as you exhale.

18. Breathe in and out slowly three times, feeling the breath come in through the soles of your feet and then flow through your body and out the top of your head.

19. Slowly open your eyes if they were closed and stretch your body.

Helping Your Partner Practice Alternative Thoughts

Jon Kabat-Zinn, widely renowned for promoting mindfulness in Western cultures, tells an interesting story about how monkeys are caught in India: "Hunters will cut a hole in a coconut that is just big enough for a monkey to put its hand through. Then they will drill two smaller holes in the other end, pass a wire through, and secure the coconut to the base of the tree. Then they put a banana inside the coconut and hide. The monkey comes down, puts his hand in and takes hold of the banana. The hole is crafted so that the open hand can go in but the fist cannot get out. All the monkey has to do to be free is let go of the banana. But it seems most monkeys don't let go" (1990, 39).

Jon Kabat-Zinn uses this example to illustrate how our minds work: we get so caught up in a particular thought or emotion that we can't let go, even though letting go would free us of the anxiety and stress.

Your partner probably has many automatic thoughts that go through his brain regularly and cause anxiety. When you notice that your partner seems anxious, you can ask him what he's thinking about and then help him to redirect his thoughts. Have your partner either verbalize his anxious thoughts or write them down. Next, help him come up with alternative thoughts he can tell himself instead. For example, if he's thinking, *I'm so anxious that I'm going to panic when I go out in public*, you might generate alternative thoughts such as *I have succeeded in overcoming this situation before, and I can do it again* or *I have the skills to not let this anxiety get the best of me.*

Think of yourself as a coach, and gently encourage your partner to repeat the positive thoughts to himself both before and during the stressful situation. You can also ask your partner the following questions:

1. What is the evidence that what you're anxious about will actually happen?

2. On a scale of 0 to 10, how strongly do you believe what you're thinking about will happen?

3. Are your thoughts taking the whole picture into account? Is there anything you might be missing?

4. How does thinking this way help you? Can you let it go?

5. How can we work together to make this less anxiety provoking?

Supporting Your Partner in Practicing Affirmations

Another way to shift thinking from anxiety to confidence is by repeating affirmations. Your partner developed a pattern of anxious thinking after having certain unhelpful thoughts repeatedly. It will take the same kind of repetition, or practice, to replace them with thoughts that are supportive and affirming. Ideally, your partner would develop a list of affirmations and then decide on two or three to work with at a time. Affirmations should be short, use positive words, and be stated in the present tense. Here are some examples of affirmations:

- *I can learn to cope with this anxiety.*

- *I'm learning to let go of my fears.*

- *When I'm feeling anxious, I can make decisions about moving toward calm.*

- *I'm able to let go of worry thoughts.*

- *I'm gaining confidence in myself.*

You can help your partner practice affirmations by taking turns stating them. First say the affirmation to your partner, stating it in the second person; for example, "You're learning to overcome your anxiety." Your partner should respond, "Yes, I am." Repeat this, you stating the affirmation and your partner replying with "Yes, I am," until you feel your partner truly believes what he's saying. Then switch roles, with your partner saying to you, "I'm learning to overcome my anxiety," and you replying, "Yes, you are," until you're convinced that your partner believes what he's saying.

Abdominal Breathing

Since our breath is automatic, we generally don't give it much thought unless we're struggling to breathe for some reason. However, paying attention to the breath is important, especially for people who have anxiety. When we're stressed, our breath becomes shallower and we tend to breathe from the chest. This way of breathing can heighten anxiety symptoms. It can also lead to hyperventilation, which can feel very similar to a panic attack.

Breathing from the abdominal area, on the other hand, increases the amount of oxygen available to the brain and muscles, stimulates the parasympathetic nervous system (which calms us from a state of arousal), improves concentration, and can help us relax (Bourne 2005). Devoting just a bit of time to focusing on the breath and breathing from the abdomen can be enormously beneficial. Here are some instructions on exactly how to go about it:

1. While sitting or lying comfortably, place one hand on your chest and one hand on your abdomen. Breathing normally, notice which hand rises when you breathe in.

2. On your next inhalation, breathe deeply so that the hand on your abdomen rises. Inhale through your nose for a count of four, counting the numbers to yourself slowly as you inhale: "One... two... three... four."

3. After inhaling, pause for a count of four.

4. Exhale slowly, through either your nose or your mouth, for a count of at least five.

5. After exhaling fully, take two breaths as you would normally.

6. Repeat steps two through five. Continue this cycle for three to five minutes.

Practiced on a daily basis, this technique will promote calm and help retrain breathing patterns. It's also helpful in a crisis; if your partner feels anxiety and panic rising, abdominal breathing will redirect his focus from his anxious thoughts to his breath, and when done correctly, it creates a calming sensation.

Progressive Muscle Relaxation

Does your partner often complain that he feels tense or uptight, or that he can't relax? This is common among people with anxiety, who often experience chronic tightness in the chest, neck, back, and shoulders. Progressive muscle relaxation (PMR) can help. PMR is a process of tightening and releasing different muscle groups throughout the body. You tense each group tightly and hold the tension for a few seconds, and then suddenly release, allowing the feeling of relaxation to spread through the muscle group. By systematically working your way through all of the major muscle groups, you can help your entire body relax and release any pent-up tension.

When practiced regularly, PMR is an effective technique for reducing the muscle tension often associated with stress and anxiety. It can also help with stress or tension headaches, migraines, backaches, and jaw tightness. If your partner practices PMR daily for at least twenty minutes each time, he's likely to feel an increased sense of relaxation that lasts long after the practice is over.

Before I explain the specifics of PMR, here are some general guidelines:

- Allow at least twenty minutes to do this exercise. Find a quiet place to relax that is free of distractions and interruptions. It may be helpful to establish a routine in which you practice PMR at the same time each day.

- Find a comfortable position that includes having your head supported. If you're feeling sleepy, sitting up rather than lying down can help prevent falling asleep. If you lie down, having a pillow under your knees can provide support.

- Loosen any tight clothing and remove your watch, jewelry, shoes, glasses, and so on.

- Adopt the mind-set that whatever happens, happens, and that you aren't going to worry about anything during this time. Don't try to force yourself to relax or not worry. Just do your best to accept your experience and let go.

- If you have any muscle areas that have been injured or feel painful when tensed, feel free to omit those areas from this exercise.

Until you get familiar with this exercise, it may be helpful to have someone read the following script to you as you practice or to record it and listen as you practice. The following exercise is adapted from *The Anxiety and Phobia Workbook* (Bourne 2005):

1. Begin by taking three full abdominal breaths, exhaling slowly and fully each time. During each exhalation, imagine tension being released from your body.

2. Clench your fists, holding them squeezed tight for seven to ten seconds. Then release and relax for fifteen to twenty seconds. Notice the difference in sensations between tension and relaxation. As you proceed through all of the following muscle groups, continue to use these same time intervals and to focus on the difference in sensations.

3. Tighten your biceps by bending your elbows and bringing your hands toward your shoulders. Hold for seven to ten seconds, then release for fifteen to twenty seconds and notice the difference in sensations.

4. Tighten your triceps by straightening your arms and locking your elbows. Hold for seven to ten seconds, then release.

5. Tense the muscles in your forehead by raising your eyebrows as high as possible. Hold for seven to ten seconds, then release.

6. Tense the muscles around your eyes by clenching your eyelids tightly shut. Hold for seven to ten seconds, then release.

7. Tighten your jaw by opening your mouth wide enough that the muscles around your jaw are stretched. Hold for seven to ten seconds, then release.

8. Tighten the muscles of your neck by tilting your head back, as though looking at the ceiling if you're sitting or at the wall behind you if you're lying down. Hold for seven to ten seconds, then release. (You may want to repeat this step, as the neck can be extra tight.)

9. Take a few abdominal breaths and focus on relaxing your neck and letting your head sink into whatever it's resting on.

10. Tighten your shoulders by raising them up toward your ears. Hold for seven to ten seconds, then release.

11. Tighten your shoulder blades by pushing them back toward your spine. Hold for seven to ten seconds, then release. (You may want to repeat this step as well, since the shoulders are another area where people often hold tension.)

12. Tighten your chest muscles by taking a full breath into your chest and expanding it. Hold for seven to ten seconds, then release.

13. Tighten your stomach muscles by sucking in your stomach. Hold for seven to ten seconds, then release.

14. Tighten your lower back by arching it. Hold for seven to ten seconds, then release. (Omit this step if you have low back pain.)

15. Tighten your buttocks by squeezing them together. Hold for seven to ten seconds, then release.

16. Tighten your thigh muscles. Hold for seven to ten seconds, then release.

17. Tighten your calf muscles by flexing your feet so your toes point up toward your body. Hold for seven to ten seconds, then release.

18. Tighten your feet by curling your toes down. Hold for seven to ten seconds, then release.

19. Scan your body for any remaining tension. Repeat the appropriate step to release any tension.

20. Imagine a wave of relaxation spreading through your body, starting from your head and moving through every muscle in your body.

21. Slowly open your eyes and return your attention to the world around you.

Visualization

Visualization is a good way for anyone to de-stress and relax. For your partner, it can also allow him to mentally remove himself from an anxious situation and become calm without striving to overcome the anxiety. With visualization, all he's trying to do is turn off the anxious thoughts so he can refocus on what's important and envision success.

Professional athletes use visualization to prepare for an event, imagining themselves crossing the finish line of the track and seeing a new personal record on the time clock; seeing the ball leave the pitcher's hand and then seeing themselves swinging the bat and watching the ball sail over the fence; or mentally practicing free throws, imagining bouncing the ball on the court and the movement to release the ball, and seeing it sink through the net. Here are some instructions for doing a visualization using the senses of smell, hearing, touch, and sight:

1. Make yourself comfortable in a place where you can relax without interruptions.

2. Visualize yourself in a peaceful scene that you can vividly see in your mind—a place that feels safe and calming to you. It can be a real place or somewhere imagined. Some suggestions are a meadow, a beach, a forest, or a garden, but pick whatever works for you.

3. Close your eyes and imagine yourself in this safe, calming place. Since this place is in your mind, it's easily accessible twenty-four hours a day, seven days a week.

4. Imagine the smells of the place. What scents are associated with it? Flowers? Suntan lotion? Damp leaves? Fresh air? Grass?

5. Imagine the sounds of the place. Are there waves crashing or birds singing? Are leaves rustling? Can you hear insects buzzing, or is it just quiet?

6. Imagine what being in that place feels like. Is there warm sun on your face? Is a breeze blowing? Is it misty or damp? Is it cool, comfortable, or warm?

7. Explore the place visually. How many different colors can you see? What are the shapes around you? Is it bright or dim? Are there shadows? Can you see the sky? Are there clouds? What do they look like? Are there plants or creatures around?

8. When you feel relaxed, slowly open your eyes and gently bring yourself back to your surroundings. Remember that you can visit this special place any time you need a break.

What's Next?

All of the techniques in this chapter can be helpful for both you and your partner. In addition to helping relieve your partner's anxiety in the moment, they can help reduce anxiety levels in the long term and will promote calm and relaxation. Figuring out which work for each of you and practicing those techniques regularly will create an excellent foundation for the approaches you'll learn in the next chapter—techniques targeted to different types of anxiety.

CHAPTER 6

Responding to Specific Types of Anxiety

As you know from reading previous chapters, anxiety can manifest in many ways, running the gamut from low-level "everyday" anxiety to full-blown panic attacks and all-consuming anxiety that prevents people from living fulfilling, productive lives. Because of this, and because the experience of anxiety is so individualized, there isn't a one-size-fits-all approach to neutralizing anxiety, though the techniques in chapter 5 will certainly be helpful for anyone who struggles with anxiety.

Fortunately, there are numerous interventions that can be very helpful for specific anxiety disorders and different types of anxiety, and I'll outline some of the most effective approaches in this chapter.

I'll begin by explaining how you can assess what's happening with your partner during acute anxiety, meaning anxiety that arises suddenly. In this situation, a quick intervention can often resolve the problem. Next I'll explain how to address chronic anxiety using exposure therapy, a highly effective method for helping people overcome their fear of specific objects or situations. Then I'll discuss strategies specific to each of the six anxiety disorders and that include case examples to illustrate how couples have used those approaches in their relationship.

As you read through this chapter, continue to practice the techniques in chapter 5. Then, after trying the techniques in this chapter that are appropriate to your partner's anxiety, you'll have a good idea of what works and what doesn't. This will be invaluable information in creating a plan for how you can respond effectively when anxiety strikes.

Addressing Acute Anxiety: CARE

When anxiety strikes suddenly, perhaps out of the blue, you need to approach the situation like a first responder at an accident scene, rapidly assessing what's happening with your partner and deciding on a course of action. Here's an acronym that can help you remember what to do in an acute anxiety situation—CARE:

> **C:** Be **c**alm and **c**ompassionate. Above all else, and no matter what happens, remain calm and be compassionate. This will allow you to provide appropriate support if necessary, and if desired by your partner. If you get angry, frustrated, or anxious, that won't improve the situation. Just remember that accommodating your partner's anxiety isn't a compassionate move, even if it seems like it in the moment. Her anxiety won't improve in the long run if you simply step in and make an accommodation.

> **A:** **A**ssess your partner's symptoms. How do you know your partner is experiencing anxiety? What signs, symptoms, and signals is she showing? Because the severity of anxiety can range so widely, you should choose an intervention

appropriate to what your partner is feeling. Some forms of anxiety require more deliberate interventions than others. (You'll learn more about this as you read through this chapter.)

R: Reinforce and **r**emind. Your partner is probably already trying to reduce her anxiety on her own. If so, give positive reinforcement about what she's tried. If she hasn't tried anything yet and seems to be unable or unwilling to help herself, remind her of techniques that have been effective in reducing her anxiety. (In addition to those you learned in chapter 5, you'll learn more in this chapter.) When your partner tries one or more of the suggested techniques, praise her and use your empathy skills to express your understanding of how difficult it must have been to handle this challenge.

E: Evaluate. After some time has passed (how much time depends on the severity of the anxiety), evaluate the situation. Is your partner's anxiety level improving? If yes, let things be and continue to offer support and encouragement. If your partner's anxiety level isn't decreasing, start over again: Make sure you're acting in a calm and compassionate manner, and then repeat the steps of assessing, reinforcing and reminding, and evaluating.

Addressing Chronic Anxiety: Exposure Therapy

The CARE approach is very effective in acute anxiety situations when your partner needs a quick intervention to help neutralize her feelings and allow her to return to a calmer state. For long-term, chronic anxiety, many people consider exposure therapy to be the gold standard of treatment. It's used by mental health professionals to treat many types of anxiety. Depending on the severity of your partner's anxiety and your comfort level with being a support person, exposure therapy may be something you and your partner want to try on your own, although it's generally best to use this technique under the guidance of a trained professional. As the name indicates, during exposure therapy, your partner will be exposed to situations that generate anxiety in order to help her learn that she can actually tolerate the anxiety and even reduce it so that the feared situation becomes manageable, and eventually perhaps neutral or even enjoyable.

Exposure therapy is conducted by creating a hierarchy of situations that provoke increasing amounts of anxiety. Starting with the least challenging situation, your partner will be encouraged to stay in each situation until her anxiety decreases. Once this becomes manageable, she'll move on to the next step in the hierarchy. If a situation proves to be too anxiety provoking, she can return to a previous step and wait for the anxiety to subside before working on the next step again.

Let's say your partner has a fear of heights but wants to be able to visit the observatory at the top of the Empire State Building during an upcoming trip to New York City with friends. Right now, anytime she looks out a window above the third floor of a building, she starts sweating, gets nauseous, and feels dizzy. Her exposure hierarchy might look something like this:

1. Look out the window from the ground floor of a building for one minute.

2. Go to the second floor of a building with a support person and look out a window for one minute. If any anxiety symptoms arise, she can use the breathing and imagery techniques described in chapter 5 until she feels better.

3. Look out the second-floor window for two to five minutes, still with a support person present.

4. Look out and down from a second-floor window for one to two minutes without a support person present.

5. Repeat steps three and four on the third floor, then the fourth floor, and so on, moving up two to three floors per session. At first, sessions should last no more than thirty minutes, and the duration can be shorter if your partner reaches a point where her anxiety is too intense.

6. At the beginning of the next session, your partner should start on the floor below where the previous session ended. So if she ended the previous session on the fifth floor, she should start the next session on the fourth floor. If the fourth floor is too overwhelming as a starting place, she can start on the third floor instead.

7. Your partner continues in this way, moving up floor by floor, until she feels more relaxed about heights. Once the fear of looking out of high windows is under control, she can add a new challenge; for example, working on being comfortable on an outdoor balcony, rooftop garden, or fire escape.

Sometimes people find that they are unable to master and move beyond a particular item on their hierarchy—for example, your partner might find it impossible to get above the twelfth floor despite repeated attempts. In this case, it may be that adjusting the hierarchy to include some intermediate steps will help.

The purpose of exposure therapy is not just to eliminate a particular fear, but to teach people that they can tolerate discomfort and give them an opportunity to practice techniques for reducing anxiety in a safe and controlled environment. What seems like an insurmountable fear can be broken down into smaller steps that can be mastered, eventually leading to freedom from the fear.

Disorder-Specific Interventions

The following sections describe disorder-specific strategies for responding to anxiety. If your partner has been diagnosed with a particular anxiety disorder, the two of you can try the approach described in that section. Even if your partner has not been diagnosed with a specific anxiety disorder, reading through the following sections will still be worthwhile. The techniques and case examples may give you ideas about additional ways to help your partner with her anxiety. By the way, the communication skills you learned in chapter 4 will probably prove invaluable as the two of you implement these strategies.

While these strategies can be very effective, it's also essential to seek help from a mental health professional who is trained in treating anxiety. Your partner's therapist will take a thorough history of your partner's symptoms and develop a treatment plan specifically tailored to her needs. The therapist may ask that you attend several sessions with your partner so that you will also be informed about the treatment and how you can help support the goals of treatment in day-to-day life, outside of sessions. The therapist may also recommend that your partner consider medications to alleviate anxiety symptoms. It's best to work with a psychiatrist on medications, as they tend to be more well-informed about appropriate antianxiety medications and dosages.

Panic Disorder with Agoraphobia

If your partner has panic disorder with agoraphobia, it's likely that the two of you have developed a pattern in which you typically accompany your partner on forays outside your home, and that you've taken on the responsibility for shopping, errands, and other tasks that require leaving the house.

Being by your partner's side when she's out in public allows her to rely on you to provide a sense of safety. Without you, she may feel as if the possibility of having an embarrassing panic attack in public is a genuine threat. However, as discussed, this kind of accommodation is actually counterproductive in the long run. It may seem like a way to show care and concern for your partner, but it prevents her from learning that she can overcome her anxiety and live a full life. An approach based on exposure therapy can help change this pattern so that your partner becomes less dependent on you:

1. Identify the responsibilities you've taken on that your partner needs to regain confidence about handling herself, such as shopping, driving the kids to school, or attending appointments alone.

2. Create a hierarchy of activities from those that seem easiest for your partner to accomplish to most challenging. (An example hierarchy for fear of heights appeared earlier in the chapter, and you'll find another example later in this chapter in the section on specific phobias.)

3. Work together to decide what steps need to be taken to tackle the first item on the hierarchy. For example, let's say the first item is for your partner to take over grocery shopping again. The two of you would then work through a series of exposures to the grocery store to help your partner learn to manage her anxiety and eventually feel confident enough to go alone. (The following case example, of Kathy and Tyler, demonstrates this approach.)

4. The two of you would then complete three steps for each of the exposures:

1. Prepare for the stressful situation ahead of time, discussing your goals, the feelings each of you are having about the upcoming exposure, any difficulties that might arise during the exposure, and how you'll handle them.

2. While in the stressful situation, your partner should express her feelings to you instead of trying to avoid unpleasant emotions. Your role is to listen, validate, and encourage your partner to ride out her feelings until they pass. If both of you feel your partner needs to leave the situation, you can take a time-out, but you shouldn't leave the situation altogether. Once your partner uses some calming techniques, reenter the situation.

3. Once the two of you are home again, discuss the experience. Each of you should describe your experience, give praise for what was accomplished, and discuss anything that needs to go differently next time.

5. As your partner develops more confidence, your role in the outings will decrease, but your partner should continue to discuss her experiences with you so you're aware of her progress and so you can offer ongoing encouragement.

• Case Example: Kathy and Tyler

Kathy, forty-two, and Tyler, forty-four, have been together for twelve years. Kathy developed panic disorder with agoraphobia after having a panic attack in public five years ago. Since then, the environment in which she feels she can function independently got progressively smaller, to the point where she rarely left the house without Tyler at her side. In therapy, Kathy has been working on learning to manage the physiological symptoms of her anxiety. The next step is for her to start relearning how to be in public without Tyler at her side. She and Tyler made a list of activities that she needs to reengage in, and together they decided that the first one to work on was decreasing her avoidance of grocery shopping.

Kathy and Tyler decided they would make their first outing to the grocery store on a Tuesday evening, since that tended to be a quiet time at their local store. Once they got there, they would just walk through the front of the store together slowly, and they would leave after five minutes. Before they left home, they discussed their plans for the outing and their feelings about it. Kathy rated her anxiety level at 6 on a scale of 0 to 10. She and Tyler decided that they would monitor her anxiety level while they were in the store and take a time-out if she reached a 9. Tyler told Kathy that he felt good about Kathy's ability to be successful during this outing.

When they arrived at the store, Kathy said she felt that her anxiety level was at 7. They sat in the car for a few minutes, and Kathy practiced some deep breathing techniques to reduce her anxiety. When she felt her anxiety was at 5, they got out of the car and approached the store, side by side but not touching each other in any way (holding hands, linking arms, and so on). They went through the doors and stepped to the side so they wouldn't be in the way but would still be inside the store. Kathy rated her anxiety level at 6. As they stood just inside the door, Kathy quietly verbalized her feelings, and Tyler encouraged her to keep at it. Kathy's anxiety peaked at 7. When the five minutes was up, they left the store and drove home.

Once they arrived back home, they discussed their experience and made plans for the next outing. They agreed that next time they would go farther into the store, stay longer (ten minutes), and, for a few minutes, spend time at opposite ends of an aisle so that Kathy could see Tyler was nearby but begin to learn that he didn't have to be right with her at all times.

Obsessive-Compulsive Disorder

Assisting your partner in overcoming OCD behaviors largely revolves around two key strategies: not participating in the behaviors yourself, and consistently encouraging your partner not to engage in the behaviors. Although it might alleviate your partner's distress in the moment if you, for example, check the stove and make sure all of the small appliances are unplugged, doing so actually reinforces her fears.

If you've been trying to alleviate your partner's fears by giving continual reassurance or arguing that her fears are illogical, you need to stop that behavior as well. Not only is it ineffective in relieving your partner's distress, it's also likely to make you frustrated and angry with her.

• Case Example: Brian and Paul

Brian, thirty-two, and Paul, thirty-five, have been partners for four years. When they met, Brian had been experiencing some symptoms of OCD for as long as he could remember, including a fear that the stove or oven would be left on or that an appliance in the house would accidentally spark a fire. During the first few years of their relationship, Paul tried his best to reassure Brian that everything was fine when they were out of the house, but he often found himself returning home with Brian to check on the house. Over time, Paul became more and more frustrated with Brian's fears and how they affected their ability to be social and live full lives.

Paul finally convinced Brian that he needed to work with a mental health professional to address his obsessions. He attended several sessions with Brian so he could learn how to best support Brian in his recovery. With the therapist, they discussed patterns of behavior they were engaging in to accommodate Brian's anxiety and agreed on ways to gradually reduce Paul's accommodations. For example, if they were out shopping and Brian became anxious about the stove not being turned off, Paul would say, "I appreciate that you're concerned about the stove being on. I understand that you'd like us to go home and check, but we agreed that the best thing to do is to help you learn to manage these feelings that you're having instead." Another behavior they agreed to work on changing was Paul's reactions to Brian's requests that they check the appliances in the kitchen "one more time" after leaving the house but before getting in the car to depart, which Paul had been accommodating in the hope that doing so would prevent Brian from later insisting that they return home to check on things. They decided that they wouldn't do that final check, and that if Brian became anxious, they would practice abdominal breathing together as they drove to their destination to help Brian calm down. With time and practice, Brian's fears lessened significantly, as did Paul's frustration level.

Generalized Anxiety Disorder

People who have GAD may seem similar to those who have OCD in that they have frequent fears that aren't alleviated by continual reassurance, and their fears are often things that many people worry about, such as finances, job security, or health problems, but blown out of proportion. People with GAD often catastrophize, taking their worries to an extreme level and assuming that the worst will always happen, even if the actual probability is quite low. If you have a partner with GAD, trying to remain calm and provide reassurance, despite your words not helping, can wear you down. You may finally reach a point where you decide you aren't going to try to help your partner feel better, given that it doesn't make any difference when you try to do so. In addition, people with GAD often have physical complaints, such as headaches and an upset stomach, that can interfere with emotional and sexual intimacy. Listening to a partner's continual complaints about these symptoms can also become annoying.

Couples in which one person has GAD often go to therapy because of the underlying tension the anxious partner's thoughts and behaviors are causing in the relationship. The therapist often provides psychoeducation, teaching both partners about GAD, and helps the couple examine the patterns in their relationship that maintain or exacerbate the anxiety. For example, some people develop GAD because they feel their partner is closing them out from participating in major decisions, such as how money is spent or invested, or feel that their partner makes all the decisions for the family and neglects to consult them or consider their opinion first.

Another issue is that people with GAD may develop a fear of inadequacy and believe that nothing they do is good enough for their partner or family. As a result, they might overcompensate by trying to make everything perfect all of the time, or underperform, not doing anything because they believe their efforts will be judged as wrong. Since GAD is a form of chronic anxiety, a therapist will help both partners look for long-standing issues that are fueling the anxiety and help get to the heart of the issue so that changes can be made, if possible. These changes might show up in many areas of life, including money concerns, health issues, levels of responsibility for family matters, job stress, sexual dissatisfaction, differences in parenting styles, and poor communication skills, to name just a few.

The therapist might also teach both partners cognitive restructuring, a technique that involves changing thoughts. This approach involves learning to recognize thoughts that are increasing anxiety and then challenging the anxious thoughts by assessing the likelihood that the anxiety-provoking event will actually occur. If your partner has GAD, her therapist may have her practice whatever is causing her anxiety during their sessions together, such as rehearsing a speech, making phone calls, or going out in public together, in order to assess the level of anxiety generated and practice challenging the thoughts that arise. The therapist may also ask your partner to keep a thought record or thought log between sessions that they can use to identify patterns and discuss alternative perspectives on whatever is fueling your partner's anxiety. The technique of helping your partner practice alternative thoughts (described in chapter 5) will also be useful here.

• Case Example: Beth and Dan

Beth, fifty-five, and Dan, fifty-six, have been married for over thirty years. Beth is a self-described worrier who has always been concerned about the kids, finances, and the future. Dan has joked many times over the years that if he wants to know the worst-case scenario in any situation, Beth will have an answer. Now that their children are grown and out of the house, Beth and Dan have been redefining their relationship, and without the distraction of children, tension between them has been increasing because Dan can seldom escape from Beth's near-constant fretting.

At Dan's encouragement, Beth started seeing a therapist, who has helped her learn to challenge her worrisome thoughts, doing reality testing to assess how realistic her fears are. At the therapist's request, Dan attended several sessions so that the three of them could discuss long-standing patterns in the relationship that are maintaining Beth's anxiety and devise ways to change. The therapist encouraged Dan to be empathetic and gentle when helping Beth challenge her fears; for example, by saying something like "I hear that you're worried about the kids traveling at night, but they've been safe drivers for many years, and there's little reason to believe tonight will be different." The therapist also encouraged Beth and Dan to do relaxing and enjoyable activities together, both to relieve Beth's anxiety symptoms and to bring them closer together as a couple. They now regularly take walks on the trails near their home and go out on dates, and they're making plans for travel after they retire. Recently, Dan has noticed that Beth is less anxious in general, and that she's better able to challenge her thoughts when her anxiety is increasing.

Social Phobia

As discussed in chapter 1, social phobia can take many different forms. To name just a few, it can prevent your partner from engaging in social activities, make going to work difficult, or lead to problems in creating and maintaining relationships. One of the techniques therapists use to help clients overcome social phobia is conducting experiments in which the person tries a feared behavior and examines the results. For example, if your partner is afraid of attending parties because of a fear of rejection, her therapist might ask her to go to a party and bring back examples of being rejected. If your partner has none to report, that provides data they can work with in session. They might discuss whether there was anything different about this party that resulted in your partner not feeling rejected, or whether perhaps your partner altered her behavior in some way to make herself more "acceptable."

If your partner does come back with examples of feeling rejected, this also provides data that she and her therapist can examine to evaluate whether she genuinely was rejected or simply perceived that she was. If it appears that she was rejected, they can work on social skills that will help her avoid being rejected in the future. If it appears that she wasn't, the therapist can help your partner try to figure out what actually did happen so she might better interpret the behavior of others and consider whether there might be other reasons why she feels rejected.

If your partner has social phobia, it will be very helpful if you encourage her to test her hypotheses instead of avoiding social situations. Help her see that, no matter what the outcome, she won't be a "loser" because she'll be gathering information that can lead to positive changes. If she finds that her fears didn't materialize, that's good information; then she can start examining why she predicts negative outcomes that don't actually happen. If the feared situation did occur, you can work together to examine what happened and come up with a plan to prevent it from occurring again or devise a plan to help your partner better cope if the situation does arise in the future.

• Case Example: Jon and Judy

Jon, who is fifty-five, has been a hospital administrator at a large academic institution for over twenty years. He's recently transitioned into a new role and is losing sleep at night because of his anxiety. His partner, Judy, who is forty-eight, also works at the hospital as an administrator, but in a different department. Although Jon is well educated, has been successful throughout his career, and has won awards for his service and leadership, he still worries that eventually his supervisors will decide he's incompetent and incapable of doing his job. Whenever he has to chair a meeting, he prepares for days in advance and tosses and turns all night in nervous anticipation of something going wrong, such as not being prepared to answer a question or being challenged by a coworker. After the meeting, he agonizes over perceived mistakes, even if everything went smoothly. When he has to meet with the board of trustees to report on activities in his department, he sometimes works himself into such a frenzy over his fears of what could go wrong that he vomits before or after the meeting.

Although Judy is very proud to have a partner in such an important role and often hears praise from others about the terrific job Jon does, she knows that his anxiety is taking a toll on his physical and mental health. It's also interfering with their time as a couple because Jon often works late into the evening and on weekends in an effort to ensure everything is perfect.

Recently, Jon and Judy have decided to make some changes to help Jon stop the obsessive worries that are leading to his social phobia. First, Jon has learned that physical exercise is a good outlet for his worry, so he's started going for a thirty-minute run most mornings. Some evenings he and Judy take a walk together to unwind from the stresses of the day. When Jon feels his anxiety increasing at work, he sometimes takes a fifteen-minute break to get outside in the fresh air. Other times he walks over to Judy's office to surprise her, which she always appreciates, and the distraction of doing something that's nice for both of them helps Jon refocus his thoughts.

When he starts to feel incompetent, Jon looks at the awards hanging on his office walls and reminds himself that he is truly worthy of holding his new job. He also writes out a to-do list, which helps him organize his thoughts and feel more in control of what needs to be accomplished. He shares his lists with Judy, and she gives him positive feedback about what he's completed.

As for Judy, she plans fun activities for the evenings and weekends to give Jon incentive to get home to participate, and also to provide a pleasurable distraction that helps take his mind off work. In addition, Judy encourages Jon to challenge his thoughts about failure and incompetence and reminds him to conduct experiments to determine whether his fears are valid. When Jon returns home with his data, Judy uses validation to empathize with Jon's feelings and gently challenges him to find alternative ways to interpret the events. Jon's anxiety about his work performance has improved greatly, and going to work has become fun for him again. Both Jon and Judy have noticed that their relationship has improved because of the time they're spending together doing fun activities, without work worries interfering.

Post–Traumatic Stress Disorder

If your partner has experienced a trauma that resulted in the development of PTSD, every facet of your relationship may be affected. Triggers that remind your partner of the event can happen spontaneously, catching both of you off guard, or routinely, which may call for changes in your partner's routine or your shared living situation. If your partner enters a dissociative state when remembering the trauma—meaning she becomes disconnected from what's happening in the environment around her—she may not recognize you as who you are or may become unresponsive to you. In addition, if the traumatic event occurred after the two of you became a couple, your partner's behaviors may change in unpredictable and frightening ways. All of these situations require special attention in order to relieve your partner's distress, and to keep you safe as well.

Try to remember that when your partner's PTSD is triggered, her actions and reactions don't necessarily reflect how she truly feels about you or the relationship. For example, people with PTSD often experience emotional numbing and struggle to feel positive emotions, including happiness and love. It isn't that your partner doesn't love you; rather, she might not be capable of expressing her emotions as you might expect, such as by hugging or kissing you or wanting to have sex. Another issue is that your partner may be concerned that if she interacts with others, her upsetting thoughts and feelings may come out and make others feel uncomfortable. Using the communication skills of validation and empathy is extremely important in helping your partner feel safe and understood.

If your partner's PTSD is triggered by places, events, sights, sounds, smells, or other specific experiences, this is one exception to the rule of not accommodating for anxiety. With professional treatment, your partner may become less sensitive to triggers and learn coping skills. But if you know, for example, that driving past the place where an assault occurred or watching news stories about war is going

133

to upset your partner, then don't do it. In time, your partner may become less sensitive to these triggers, but only with the help of professional treatment.

• Case Example: Jody and Gary

On a rainy night about a month ago, Jody, age thirty-three, was involved in a head-on collision while driving home from work. Both cars were totaled, and Jody had to be extricated from her car by emergency workers. The other driver, who was at fault, was hospitalized with his injuries. Jody suffered a broken wrist and a concussion from the airbags, as well as multiple cuts and bruises. When her husband Gary, age thirty-seven, arrived at the emergency room, Jody was hysterical. She knew the accident wasn't her fault and that both she and the other driver would be okay, but she told Gary that she never wanted to drive again.

Gary tried to calm her down, reassuring her that they would get her a new car—whatever she wanted that would make her feel safe—and that in a few days she would feel better. But Jody is still having nightmares about the accident and refuses to go shopping for a new car. She insists that Gary drive her to work, and not along the route she was traveling on the night of the accident, even though the alternative takes fifteen minutes longer. And even though her bruises are gone, her concussion is resolved, and her wrist is healing, she isn't interested in going out socially, either with Gary or with friends. To Jody, it seems like no one can understand what she went through, and she always feels as if she's about to start crying.

Gary began to suspect that Jody may have PTSD, so he educated himself about how he might be helpful. He learned that patience, encouragement, and understanding are the keys to being supportive when a partner has PTSD, and that it takes time to resolve the psychological damage that was done. He's been accommodating Jody's request to be driven everywhere, despite his concern that the longer he does this, the harder it will be for Jody to get behind the wheel again. He's also been gently encouraging Jody to take his car to run errands and remaining patient when she refuses. Gary hopes that his gentle nudging will eventually result in Jody deciding that it's safe to drive again. When Jody wakes up from a nightmare, Gary offers reassurances that she's safe and that it was just a dream, and he listens if Jody wants to share what she was dreaming about, but often she just wants to be held for a few minutes before falling back to sleep. Gary has also suggested that Jody go out with friends or, if going out in public feels like too much, that they could host friends at their house. In addition, he's been encouraging Jody to seek professional help from a therapist who specializes in PTSD. He helped her find a therapist and set up an initial meeting and plans to attend Jody's first session so that he can learn more about how he can help.

Specific Phobias

If your partner has a specific phobia, the most effective way she can overcome it is to face it, despite how impossible that may feel to her and how difficult it may be for you as the supportive partner. You've probably witnessed how your partner reacts in situations that trigger the phobia, and if so, you undoubtedly want to avoid that ever happening again! However, treatment consisting of exposure to triggers, if planned carefully and executed correctly, can make the unthinkable possible. Earlier in this chapter I discussed exposure therapy and how to work through a hierarchy of feared situations, and that is often exactly how phobias are treated: by creating a plan in which your partner faces increasingly intense stimuli, in a safe environment, and learns to regulate her anxiety symptoms in the process.

For some fears, such as fear of heights, bridges, or dogs, it's possible to engage in real-life exposures, actually confronting the feared object or situation. But for others, such as a fear of flying or fear of contracting a disease, that may be impractical because of time, expense, or logistics. Imagery desensitization works in much the same way as exposure therapy: Your partner would create a hierarchy that starts with a nonthreatening scenario related to her phobia and proceed stepwise through increasingly difficult scenarios. Here's an example of how a hierarchy might look for someone who has a fear of flying:

1. Arriving at the airport on the day of the flight

2. Checking baggage

3. Passing through security

4. Waiting at the gate

5. Boarding the plane

6. Finding her seat

7. Strapping on her seatbelt

8. Listening to the safety instructions

9. Hearing the departure announcements, including that the doors are being secured for takeoff

10. Taxiing on the runway

11. Accelerating on the runway for takeoff

12. Feeling the plane lift off the ground

13. Experiencing turbulence in the air

14. Feeling the sensation of descending

15. Feeling the bump of landing and the vibration of the plane during braking

After creating the hierarchy, your partner would envision the scenes sequentially, working her way up the hierarchy, using the following basic steps for imagery desensitization, adapted from *The Anxiety and Phobia Workbook* (Bourne 2005):

1. Take a few minutes to get relaxed, using any technique that helps achieve that state, such as abdominal breathing, mindful breathing, or a quick body scan.

2. Visualize yourself in a peaceful scene that you can vividly see in your mind. It can be indoors, such as relaxing by a fire, or outdoors, maybe at the beach or in the woods. It can also be a place that's entirely in your imagination. Spend about one minute visualizing this peaceful scene.

3. Move to the first scene of your phobia hierarchy. Stay with this image for thirty seconds to a minute, picturing it in as much detail as possible, as if you were actually there. Imagine yourself acting calm and confident in the scene. If you feel anxious, practice abdominal breathing and try to stay with the anxiety for an additional thirty to sixty seconds. When you feel little to no anxiety, visualize the next scene in the hierarchy.

4. When you reach a level of your hierarchy where your anxiety is above a 5 on a scale of 0 to 10, stay with the scene for about one minute, then retreat to the peaceful scene and spend about one minute there to relax again. Then repeat the visualization from the hierarchy scene you left. Continue this cycle of visualizing the phobia scene for one minute, then relaxing with the peaceful scene for one minute, until the phobia scene provokes minimal anxiety.

5. If you feel your anxiety level rising above a 7, only stay with the phobia scene for about ten seconds before retreating to the

peaceful scene, then stay in the peaceful scene until you feel completely relaxed again. If a particular step in the hierarchy remains difficult to tolerate after many attempts, add an intermediate step that's more challenging than the previous level but not as difficult as the step you've been working on.

6. Continue working through your hierarchy until you can visualize the most challenging item with minimal anxiety.

Practice imagery desensitization for fifteen to twenty minutes daily, beginning each new session with the scene one step below where you stopped before—in other words, the last scene you successfully negotiated.

• Case Example: Lisa and Jennifer

Lisa and Jennifer, both twenty-five, are preparing to celebrate their three-year anniversary and have decided to take a trip to New Orleans for Mardi Gras. Unfortunately, Lisa has a fear of being in crowds. Her chest tightens, her breathing gets shallow, she feels dizzy, and she feels she must leave the situation, even if it means running away, which draws attention. They know attending the Mardi Gras festivities will mean being in crowds, so they've decided to start working on Lisa's fears at home so that they can enjoy New Orleans and the Mardi Gras celebration to the fullest.

Working together, they created a hierarchy of exposures to help reduce Lisa's anxiety about being in crowds. Since they would be together during their trip, they also discussed how Jennifer could be helpful, such as distracting Lisa by pointing out things to look at, encouraging Lisa to stay in challenging situations a few moments longer if she starts feeling anxious, and holding hands when it seems they might get separated in a crowd.

To practice exposure prior to their trip, they started by going to a shopping mall on a weekday, when there weren't many people around. They stayed in close proximity, but Lisa had to be on her own for five minutes. Next they went to a department store in the evening, which was a bit more crowded than the mall had been. They stayed in the same department but got a little further from each other and weren't always able to make eye contact, again, for just five minutes. The next step was for Jennifer to return to the car while Lisa walked around the department store on her own for ten minutes. Whenever Lisa felt anxious, she focused her attention on the products in the store and took several deep breaths. They repeated this exposure a few times during the week and then went back to the mall on a weekend when it was a lot more crowded. Once Lisa felt comfortable being in the crowded mall on her own for twenty minutes at a time, they worked toward a more challenging situation to prepare for a different type of crowd: an outdoor rock concert.

First they went to a show at a small music venue that seated about one hundred people and remained together the entire time. Next they went to a show at the same venue, but Jennifer left Lisa alone for five minutes. Next they attended a concert in a hall that seated two thousand people. Jennifer waited outside while Lisa went in alone to find their seats and then followed her in about ten minutes later. Finally, Lisa attended a show at the same two-thousand-seat venue alone. After that success, they were able to attend an outdoor rock concert together, and Lisa was able to tolerate staying in their seats alone when Jennifer went to get food or use the restroom. When it was time for their trip to New Orleans, they had practiced enough exposures that even though Lisa was overwhelmed by the crowds at times, she never felt so fearful that they needed to retreat to their hotel or leave the city altogether. They enjoyed their anniversary trip immensely.

Making a Plan for Relieving Your Partner's Anxiety

Now that you've learned a variety of techniques that can help reduce anxiety, you can create a plan for how to help your partner by making lists of what's effective and what isn't when your partner is experiencing anxiety. This way, not only will you know what to do to help your partner, you'll also have a reminder about what doesn't work. As I've emphasized, partners of people with anxiety generally mean well, but their attempts to be helpful and supportive can inadvertently make things worse. By talking this out with your partner when she's in a calm and receptive frame of mind, you'll both be on the same page about what you can do that's genuinely helpful when anxiety strikes.

You may find that you and your partner disagree about what belongs on the list of what's helpful. As discussed in chapter 3, accommodation behaviors feel very helpful to your partner, but they keep her from overcoming her anxiety, and they keep you trapped in the role of being the rescuer, which isn't healthy for either of you in the long run. You may have to explain this to your partner or, if she's aware of the problems with accommodation behaviors, remind her why they aren't actually helpful.

If your partner resists the idea of creating a list, whether because she feels it isn't necessary or because she feels some shame about the need to have such lists, consider making the lists on your own. While teamwork would be most beneficial, if that isn't possible it will still be worthwhile to do what you can on your own.

Make a List of What Works

The first step in making a list of what's effective is to talk with your partner about how you can know that she wants your assistance in lowering her anxiety levels. The need for assistance can vary greatly depending on the person and the type of anxiety she experiences. Some people may not want any help when they feel anxious, preferring to be left alone. Others may not stand a chance of lowering their anxiety level without some help. Whatever the case in your partner's situation, deciding ahead of time what she wants you to do will help her be less resistant to your offers to help when she's experiencing anxiety.

Note that it's important to be specific when making this list and to choose interventions appropriate for particular symptoms. Here's an example of what such a list might look like.

Eric's Anxiety Relief List

- *If I'm pacing the room and unable to relax, offer to go for a walk with me outside or suggest that I go by myself.*

- *If I'm ruminating about my performance at work, pick out a movie for us to watch or play a board game with me as a distraction.*

- *If I'm obsessing over whether I locked the doors at home, reassure me (once only, not multiple times) that I did and remind me that not going home to check the locks means I'm one step closer to being free from my obsessions.*

- *Mindful breathing is helpful for me when I need to calm down. Remind me to take a time-out to focus on my breathing.*

Another way to document what's effective is to decide which symptoms could mean that your support is needed, and then make a list of strategies to try. Here's what that might look like.

Becky's Anxiety Support List

Anxiety symptoms that indicate I need support: trembling hands, being unable to relax, ruminating, picking at my cuticles or biting my nails, being unable to sleep, not eating, drinking more wine than usual (more than two glasses)

Ways to be supportive:

- *Offer to listen to what I have to say.*

- *Invite me to go for a run together.*

- *Distract me with activities, such as watching funny movies, cooking, or reading magazines.*

- *Give me a back rub or massage my hands with lotion.*

- *Encourage me to go to bed at a reasonable time.*

- *Suggest I take a hot bath or shower.*

- *Offer to read a guided meditation to me.*

Make a List of What Isn't Helpful

We've all had the experience of struggling with something and having a well-meaning person try to intervene in a way that simply doesn't help. As difficult as it may be, both you and your partner need to take an honest look at patterns of behavior that don't help with her anxiety in the long run, that may be harming the relationship, and that may even be causing problems in the short term. Making a list of what doesn't work to alleviate your partner's anxiety will help you be more aware of what to avoid so you don't make the situation worse when anxiety strikes. Here's an example of how such a list might look.

Mario's List of What Isn't Helpful

- *I won't tell my partner to "get over it."*

- *I won't use guilt to make my partner stop her behavior.*

- *I won't use drugs or alcohol as a way to cope with my emotions about my partner's behavior.*

- *I won't intervene if my partner encounters something that triggers a phobia.*

- *I won't call my partner's supervisor and tell a false story about why she isn't at work.*

- *I won't participate in a cleaning ritual with my partner.*

What's Next?

Having a plan and knowing what to do—and what not to do—when anxiety strikes can help you and your partner feel more in control of your lives and your relationship. It will put you on the road to overcoming the anxiety, rather than just living with it or potentially making it worse. Defeating the anxiety will take a lot of conscious effort from both of you as you work to overcome habitual ways of interacting, but the rewards will make the work worthwhile. To help you continue your journey toward freedom from anxiety, the next chapter will look at how lifestyle factors may be influencing your partner's anxiety and offer guidance in making changes.

CHAPTER 7

Lifestyle Choices That Can Reduce Anxiety

In chapters 5 and 6, you learned a lot of strategies that can be helpful when your partner's anxiety strikes, along with some techniques to promote relaxation and a general sense of calm for both of you. As useful as those approaches are, it may be that certain lifestyle factors are playing a role in maintaining your partner's anxiety. So in this chapter, we'll look at some lifestyle changes you and your partner can make that will help reduce, or perhaps even eliminate, some of the root causes of your partner's anxiety.

As you work with your partner (and other family members, if necessary) as a team to decide what changes you'll make, you'll become a built-in support system for each other as you move toward a more healthful lifestyle. You'll also strengthen your bond as a couple or family.

In the fast-paced world we live in, the chances of living an anxiety-free life are pretty slim. Although some people seem to sail through life without a care in the world, the majority of us need to make deliberate choices and consciously apply ourselves to minimizing the stress in our lives. As mentioned in chapter 1, some anxiety is necessary for survival, serving as a signal that we need to respond to a threat to our safety. But when the intensity and duration of anxiety are at levels that are detrimental to your partner's well-being, it's important to make lifestyle changes to help turn the situation around. The simple truth is this: People who are prone to anxiety need to be especially diligent about minimizing the stress in their lives.

Some of the lifestyle changes I suggest in this chapter may seem challenging to you or your partner, but I encourage both of you to try them anyway. You can always return to old habits if you find that a particular change doesn't have the desired effect. However, I do ask that you implement each change consistently for at least thirty days to ensure that you give it a chance to make a difference.

That said, and even though I've been emphasizing working together as a team to reduce your partner's anxiety, you may not need or want to make the same lifestyle changes as your partner. If you're going to feel resentful toward your partner because of giving up your morning cup of coffee, for example, it's not a requirement that you do that. Just be aware that it's often easier to do new things when working as a team, so your participation may lend your partner needed support.

No matter who is making the changes, I recommend that you tackle them one at a time, as trying to make too many lifestyle changes at once can feel overwhelming. After you read this chapter, have a discussion with your partner about which one to tackle first. You may want to start with easier changes to help get the ball rolling. Or perhaps a more difficult change holds the potential to make a big difference, so you'd like to work on that first, despite the challenge.

There will undoubtedly be times when one or both of you wants to give up on a particular change. Letting go of old habits and patterns can be hard. When you feel like throwing in the towel, remember that you need only commit to any of these changes for thirty days.

Hang in there! The rewards of reducing the anxiety and stress in your relationship are worth it.

Foods and Beverages

Like most people, you and your partner may tend to reach for favorite comfort foods after a hard day or tell yourself you deserve a treat after a trying experience. Unfortunately, some of the foods and beverages that we tend to reach for can have a major impact on mood, due to their effects on our biochemistry.

You probably don't need a dietitian to tell you that a poor diet can affect all areas of your life, often leading to weight gain, certain diseases, insomnia, low energy levels, diminished mental health, and other negative outcomes. Any food or beverage that's nutritionally lacking can be a problem, but there are four main categories to steer clear of: caffeine, sugary foods and beverages, alcohol, and highly processed foods, for reasons I'll discuss below.

Before you throw this book across the room, saying, "You're taking all of my favorite things away," remember why it's worthwhile to commit to thirty days of trying these new habits: to reduce stress and anxiety in your relationship. However, please note that I highly recommend working with a registered dietitian before making any major dietary changes.

Caffeine

Avoiding caffeine should be a no-brainer. After all, why do people drink coffee (or other beverages with caffeine in them) in the morning? Because they want to wake up, and caffeine is a stimulant. But for people who are prone to anxiety, your partner included, stimulants can be a big problem. Excessive caffeine intake can have effects that mimic the symptoms of anxiety: increased heart rate, shakiness, and feelings of panic.

In addition, caffeine can affect sleep, and if your partner doesn't sleep well, his anxiety levels will remain high. On top of that, excessive caffeine consumption can cause a depletion of vitamin B1 (thiamine), which has been called the antistress vitamin because it improves the body's ability to withstand the effects of stress (Balch 2006). Is the coffee or tea worth it?

When eliminating caffeine, keep in mind that it can show up in other beverages and foods—some that you might not suspect. Of course, most energy drinks contain caffeine, as do many sodas. Also watch out for chocolate, certain headache medications, cocoa, and even green tea.

Candy and Simple Sugars

When we see kids running around like crazy, we often think *How much sugar have they had today?* As with caffeine, we gravitate to sweets when we need a lift in mood because that's exactly what sugar delivers. But the boost is short-lasting and results in depleted blood sugar levels afterward, often leading to a lower mood than before. In addition, low blood sugar levels can trigger hypoglycemia, a condition with symptoms that mimic a panic attack, including trembling, feelings of weakness or dizziness, heart palpitations, anxiety, lightheadedness, and irritability. In fact, some people have panic attacks that are triggered by hypoglycemia, and the panic subsides when they eat something. However, do note that the majority of people with anxiety don't have hypoglycemia, and that only medical testing can determine whether a person is experiencing blood sugar problems.

Alcohol

As mentioned earlier in the book, sometimes people with anxiety self-medicate by using alcohol to manage their symptoms. If your partner does this, setting a goal of removing all alcohol from the house and abstaining completely is a good idea.

However, keep in mind that if your partner has been self-medicating with alcohol and that crutch is removed without providing some sort of alternative, it's probably a recipe for disaster. Compassionately engage your partner in a discussion of alternatives to using alcohol to manage his symptoms, and encourage him to decrease his dependence on alcohol gradually. I also strongly recommend that you enlist professional help for your partner in transitioning away from alcohol use.

As discussed in chapter 1, another issue with alcohol is that it can interfere with any anxiety medications your partner may be taking. Alcohol is a sedative, and combining it with anxiety-reducing medications can severely impair central nervous system functioning—to the point where the vital functions of heartbeat and breathing stop. Since people often drink at night, this can happen when your partner is asleep, potentially resulting in a terrible tragedy. A few beers or that bottle of wine aren't worth the risk.

Highly Processed Foods

People who are prone to anxiety are often sensitive in many other ways as well and may react to highly processed foods and beverages, such as hot dogs, sausage, lunch meats, baked goods, sodas, and most packaged snack foods. These foods and beverages are difficult to digest—for anyone—and also tend to be low in vitamins, minerals, and other essential nutrients that help our bodies function efficiently. Working to replace highly processed foods with more natural and organic choices is a commitment, but it can be a great way to connect with your partner as both of you try, discover, and share new and healthier alternatives.

Exercise

Exercise has so many benefits, yet most people tend to resist it. Because those benefits include helping alleviate anxiety, it's especially important for your partner to engage in a program of regular physical activity.

At first glance, the changes the body experiences during exercise are the same as those produced by anxiety—sweating, rapid breathing, racing heart, faster blood circulation, and rapid fatigue. In fact, this similarity makes some people with anxiety reluctant to begin an exercise program. However, there's a difference between the two: Anxiety symptoms are gearing up the body to fight or to flee, whereas exercise can release that tension and flush out the neurotransmitters that create anxiety symptoms to prepare the body to react to the perceived threat.

If either you or your partner haven't been engaging in regular exercise and decide to start, please check with your primary care physician first, especially if either of you is overweight or has medical problems. When you begin, be sure to start slowly and work your way up to a vigorous exercise regimen gradually. If you haven't been exercising regularly and you decide to run for an hour on the first day, it's almost guaranteed that your new program won't extend to a second day. This approach will also be helpful if your partner fears exercise because it can feel physiologically similar to a panic attack. Taking it gradually and increasing the duration or intensity in small increments will serve as a form of exposure therapy.

Technology Use

Take a minute to consider how many electronic devices you and your partner use regularly. Between the two of you, you're likely to have multiple phones and at least one television, radio or other sound system, and computer. You may also regularly use gaming devices, e-readers, and iPods or other personal audio devices. Not that long ago, many of these devices didn't exist. These days, it's nearly impossible to ever "unplug," and for many people, the thought of turning off these devices and not being constantly connected causes anxiety.

If technology use is an issue for your partner, it would be a good idea to discuss it and try to determine the source of the anxiety: Is he anxious because he feels a need to be connected at all times, or does his anxiety stem from wanting to disconnect and feeling that he can't or isn't allowed to? Either way, establishing some boundaries around technology use will go a long way in reducing your partner's anxiety.

Cell Phones

It's hard to believe that, once upon a time, people actually left their homes without carrying a phone with them. In many ways, cell phones have been a blessing; it's pretty handy to be able to summon help, to let someone know you're running late, or to find out if there's anything you need to pick up at the store. But cell phones do have their downsides as well. They make us constantly available, eroding our downtime and leading to frequent interruptions, all of which can increase stress and anxiety.

Then there are the dangers involved in using a cell phone while driving. Many states have laws against using a cell phone while driving, and for good reason. Trying to talk on the phone while watching the road is difficult, no matter how practiced you are at it. Make an agreement with your partner that neither of you will use your cell phone while driving. You may have to adjust your expectations about how quickly a call will be returned. If your partner gets anxious when you don't immediately answer, he'll need to practice skills for calming himself while he waits for you to call back, such as abdominal breathing, a brief mindfulness practice, or whatever works best for him when feeling acutely anxious.

Another potential cause of anxiety is if your partner hears his phone ring while driving and makes the choice not to answer. He may become consumed with thoughts like *I wonder who that was? Should I fish the phone out of my pocket and look? What if it was important?* This one is easily solved: Encourage your partner to turn his cell phone off when driving—or anytime he doesn't want to be interrupted. This eliminates any temptation to check who's calling. Remind your partner (and yourself, if need be) that not that long ago no one had a cell phone, and it was usually okay to wait until a convenient time to return calls.

To address the impacts of cell phone use on other aspects of life beyond driving, encourage your partner to have times when he turns his phone off or chooses to ignore it and focus on something else. For example, he might decide to turn his phone off at nine o'clock each night or to turn it off when he's at work and check for messages only at lunchtime. It would also be a good idea to have a schedule for weekends that would allow both of you to check your phones regularly in case of an emergency while also giving you some breathing room so you don't feel you must always respond instantly.

Computers, Internet, and Social Media

Computers and other electronic devices can also keep us connected like never before. Social media such as Facebook and Twitter have revolutionized how we communicate. Again, this has good and bad aspects. Among the positives, we can often more easily connect with people we care about, including people we may have lost touch with. However, we also become more vulnerable to information overload. And as with cell phones, there can be a feeling that you need to be connected all the time or you might miss out on something.

Information overload can make stress and anxiety worse. Before the rise of the Internet, we generally had only limited resources for finding information: books, newspapers, television, radio, and word of mouth. Now endless sources of information from all over the world are online and instantly available. Unfortunately, for people with anxiety, having too many choices often feels overwhelming. If this is an issue for your partner, help him select a few trusted resources to get information from; for example, he might stick with just one website for news and do online shopping at only a few sites. Other approaches might be placing a limit on the amount of time spent searching for information or, better yet, asking someone who would know where to find the information.

Facebook, Twitter, and other social media outlets can be a particularly slippery slope for people who have anxiety. You and your partner will need to gauge how much influence social media has on your lives. Some people are perfectly okay with not looking at these sites regularly (or not looking at them at all), whereas others panic if they have to spend more than a few hours disconnected because they fear they'll miss out on something.

One way to test your partner's reliance on social media is to have him sign off from these sites for a certain period of time and see how he does. Does he feel relieved to be free from them, or does he find himself anxious and disconnected and wish he hadn't agreed to this experiment in the first place? Does he maybe even sneak a peek when he thinks you aren't looking? The results of this experiment will tell both of you a lot about whether his anxiety would improve with some changes in this area.

Another consideration is the time of day when your partner accesses the Internet or social media. Doing so late in the evening, and especially right before bed, can disrupt your partner's sleep if he reads something stimulating, whether it's positive or negative. Mealtime can also be problematic, causing some people to overeat and leading others to undereat or forgo eating altogether. Plus, as discussed earlier in the chapter, good nutrition is important in managing anxiety, and adding excessive stimulation or potential sources of anxiety to mealtimes needlessly won't be helpful.

Media Exposure

When was the last time you heard something good on a news program? Most stations do try to include a feel-good story or two per half hour, but the rest of the time it's mostly bad news about conflict, war, natural disasters, murder, assault, environmental crises, and the list goes on. Even if you avoid television and radio news, there are magazines, blogs, newspapers, billboards, and other media to pick up the slack. Also consider the types of shows you and your partner watch; so many popular shows focus on crime and other dark or upsetting topics.

You do have choices. Your first choice is whether to watch television at all. The time when we needed to watch television to get information is long gone. Consider conducting an experiment similar to the one described for social media. What would it be like to turn off the television for a few days or even a week? Would your partner's anxiety increase or decrease?

If you can't imagine giving television up altogether, it may be time for you and your partner to assess the type of shows you're watching. I had a client with severe anxiety who told me she was having trouble sleeping. She also said that she watched crime shows nightly, yet she hadn't seen a connection. I recommended that she switch to a comedy show, and it worked. Not only did her sleep improve, she also noticed a difference in her mood. Things we tend to overlook can often make a big difference in reducing anxiety.

Excessive Obligations

Many people have calendars crowded with work obligations, social engagements, volunteer activities, family responsibilities, and more. Being overextended or simply not having enough downtime can cause a lot of stress and anxiety. You and your partner may recognize this and want to scale back your activities, but also feel that all of your scheduled activities are essential and none can be eliminated. But as you now know, making an effort to reduce anxiety requires making deliberate choices—sometimes hard choices—and conscious effort. When you face tough decisions about scaling back your activities, just remember that the payoff is worth some sacrifices.

Work Obligations

Depending on the type of work your partner does, he may or may not have much control over many aspects of his job responsibilities. Wherever he does have choices, he should use them wisely. Here are some areas where he might consider making changes to reduce his anxiety:

- **Work hours:** Is your partner a morning person? If so, maybe going to work earlier than everyone else would give him some quiet time to settle in and help set the tone for the day. Would he benefit from having an extra day off each week, completely free from work obligations? If so, maybe he could work four ten-hour days instead of five eight-hour days. Does your partner often work late or on the weekends in hopes of catching up or getting ahead? If so, ask him to commit to leaving work on time every day for one month, even if it means not finishing everything. Other possibilities include exploring whether flextime is an option or, if your partner is a shift worker, whether a different shift might better align with his energy levels.

- **Taking breaks:** Most workplaces offer employees a certain amount of break time during the day based on the number of hours they work. However, many people either don't take the time allotted or feel they can't because their workplace culture frowns on it. Ask your partner how (or whether) he uses his break time. If he isn't taking breaks or is using that time to engage in social media or other online pursuits, he might benefit from spending that time relaxing, perhaps taking a walk outside, listening to music, or even sitting in a quiet area and doing a few minutes of mindful breathing. The techniques described in chapter 5 are effective in the workplace too!

- **Responsibilities:** Most employees have too many responsibilities and feel a lot of pressure to get everything done themselves. As discussed in the section on employment and anxiety in chapter 2, this sets up a cycle of anxiety, leading to performance problems, leading to more anxiety. Help your partner establish reasonable goals for himself, perhaps by looking at what he's expected to do and making a to-do list. If there are items that can be delegated to others, encourage your partner to hand those off.

Social Obligations

Because maintaining healthy, supportive relationships is so important, you and your partner may feel hard-pressed to make changes in your social calendar. However, social obligations that seem to drain your energy won't be helpful. The choices you and your partner make about how to spend your free time should *reduce* anxiety, not increase it. Here are some areas of your social life where you might consider making changes:

- Are there people in your life who are dragging you and your partner down instead of lifting you up? If so, can you spend less time with them?

- Have you gotten stuck in social routines that have come to feel more like a chore than fun? If so, are any of these activities optional?

- Have you and your partner been participating in volunteer activities that were once enjoyable but now feel like work? If so, it would be a good idea to scale back or perhaps take a complete break.

It can be challenging to let go of routines, especially when other people are involved. Plus, you and your partner probably don't want to hurt anyone's feelings by saying no. To risk sounding like a broken record, just keep in mind the many benefits of helping reduce your partner's anxiety.

Another issue with social or recreational activities may be that you and your partner have different ideas about what's relaxing or enjoyable. If you're an extrovert, you probably draw your energy from having other people around and doing stimulating activities; however, this may feel overwhelming for your partner. This isn't to say all people with anxiety are introverts; rather, you and your partner may simply have different levels of tolerance for stimulation. If this is the case, perhaps the healthiest thing you and your partner can do is decide which activities you want to participate in together and which might be better to engage in on your own.

All of that said, do consider whether your partner wants to avoid specific activities because of agoraphobia or social anxiety. You need not insist that he participate in an effort to get over his fears, but both of you should keep in mind the problems with accommodation and the benefits of exposure therapy and learning to face feared situations. Depending on what the activity is and how important it is that your partner participates, this might be an area to work on together.

Couple Time

In chapter 4 I discussed the importance of good, mutually supportive communication with your partner. In addition, I also recommend that both of you commit to spending quality time together. This is essential for reducing anxiety because it gives the two of you an opportunity to enjoy shared activities that are fun, relaxing, and renewing. It's difficult to be anxious when fully engaged in an activity with someone you love. As one example, consider planning regular date nights, even if you've been together for years, to give you and your partner something to look forward to, plan for, and talk about afterward.

If you and your partner have children, setting aside regular family time is important as well. This keeps everyone connected and has many benefits. For example, among children eleven to eighteen years old, frequent family meals are associated with a lower risk of smoking, drinking, and using drugs; a lower incidence of depressive symptoms and suicidal thoughts; and better grades (Eisenberg et al. 2004). Having dinner together most nights of the week, scheduling a game night or movie night, or going on weekend outings are all ways to increase positive interactions in the family, and to decrease stress and anxiety overall.

Mindfulness Practice

I introduced mindfulness in chapter 5 and am bringing it up again in this chapter because research indicates that both mindfulness and meditation can serve as a powerful antidote to anxiety. According to Edmund Bourne (2005, 423), an expert in the treatment of anxiety and stress-related disorders,

> "Meditation has repeatedly been found to reduce chronic anxiety and worry. Often the dosage of tranquilizers or other medications can be reduced if you are meditating daily. Other long-range benefits include sharpened alertness, increased energy level and productivity, decreased self-criticism, increased objectivity (the capacity to view situations nonjudgmentally), decreased dependence on alcohol, recreational drugs, and prescription drugs, increased accessibility of emotions, and heightened self-esteem and sense of identity."

While specific instructions about creating a mindfulness practice go beyond the scope of this book, as mentioned in chapter 5, you'll find many good sources of information both online and in print (see Resources). Two popular and excellent books on mindfulness meditation are *Mindfulness for Beginners* and *Wherever You Go, There You Are*, both by Jon Kabat-Zinn, the creator of a program called mindfulness-based stress reduction (MBSR), which has been proven effective for alleviating anxiety symptoms (Miller, Fletcher, and Kabat-Zinn 1995). If you do an online search for "mindfulness-based stress reduction" and the name of your city, you may find a program near you.

What's Next?

In many ways, our current culture fosters anxiety around being connected, meeting obligations, and other lifestyle choices. Because these aspects of life are so deeply interwoven into our daily routines, it takes conscious, deliberate effort to make changes in these areas. Doing so may not be easy, but it can lead to significant changes in anxiety levels. Choosing to implement the lifestyle changes recommended in this chapter, one at a time, and for a minimum of thirty days, could do wonders to reduce your partner's anxiety and improve quality of life for both of you. The next chapter, which is the final chapter in the book, is especially for you. It discusses many ways you can care for yourself and make sure your needs are being met so that you can be at your best when providing support for your partner.

CHAPTER 8

Self-Care for the Caregiver

When I first began writing a blog for the partners of those with mental illnesses on PsychCentral.com, I wanted to name it *Oxygen Mask*. Anyone who has ever flown on a plane is familiar with the safety recommendation to put your own oxygen mask on before assisting others. The concept is pretty simple: If you can't breathe, you won't be able to help others! Although the editors at PsychCentral and I eventually decided on *Partners in Wellness*, I regularly reminded my readers of the importance of self-care when providing support for a loved one, no matter what the illness may be. Truth be told, even if you aren't caring for someone else, self-care is still important!

What Is Self-Care?

Perhaps a definition of "self-care" is in order. Self-care means deliberately choosing to do things that bring pleasure, enjoyment, and rejuvenation to your life on a regular basis. These activities and experiences may be rewarding, challenging, exciting, and adventurous, or they may be quiet, calming, centering, and peaceful. The key is that they work for you and that they make you feel good physically, mentally, and emotionally.

Take a few minutes to read through this list and consider how many of these changes you'd like to see in your life:

- Better sleep

- Lower blood pressure

- Improved attitude and outlook

- Increased laughter and smiling

- Less worry

- Learning something new, such as a hobby, sport, or skill

- Fewer headaches, stomachaches, or other illnesses

- Less stress

- More relaxation

- More permission to enjoy yourself

All of this, and more, is possible if you engage in regular self-care activities.

No one else can do this for you. You have to make the choice to do things that bring you pleasure. When these activities involve being with other people, it's still up to you to make the time, show up, and participate. If being alone is how you recharge your batteries, it may be even more challenging to make and keep the commitment, since it's likely that no one else will be holding you accountable.

Why Self-Care Matters

People who are chronically burned-out usually don't put taking care of themselves at the top of the list. They generally have ready excuses about why they can't do so: their kids need them, their partner needs them, their parents need them, their employer needs them, their pets need them, their phone never stops ringing, their emails are piling up, there's no money, there are bills to pay, the house isn't clean, their car needs fixing, and the list goes on. If you're looking for an excuse to not take care of yourself, it's easy to find one. What's much more difficult is making the commitment to do what's in your best interests— and the best interests of your partner and other loved ones. Challenging as it may be, it's crucial. When you live with an anxious partner, there can be a lot of tension in your relationship and in your home. Having self-care routines and plans in place can help neutralize the static.

Getting Over the Excuses

As mentioned, people tend to have a lot of excuses for why they can't take care of themselves. Those listed above mostly involve time and conflicting obligations. However, most of us do have time for what matters to us, so with these excuses the solution is simply to move self-care to the top of your list.

Another common category of excuses is those with the theme "I don't deserve to care for myself." Such excuses can take many different forms, from "I have to work this weekend because I can never get ahead on this pile of papers" to "It's more important that I be there for the kids because my partner is struggling right now" to "I'm fine. A glass of wine [antianxiety pill, pot of coffee, bag of cookies, whatever] will make me feel better so I can keep going." While sometimes we must put self-care aside or resort to a quick fix to get through a temporary situation, doing this repeatedly over the long term isn't effective. It leads to burnout, often at the most inconvenient times. Have you ever gotten sick just before a big event or when a work deadline was looming? Chances are you were pushing the limits of your health and wellness and nature won. That can be prevented.

Sometimes people delude themselves into thinking that they are somehow immune to the problems that arise from pushing the limits of one's energy and emotional resources. Unfortunately, we all have limits, although they do vary from person to person. It's in your best interests (and the best interests of those around you) not only to recognize what your limits are but to respect them, even if it means not accomplishing everything you think you need to do or risking disappointing others. It genuinely doesn't make sense to try to work if you have pneumonia or to wash the windows when you have a migraine.

I'd like you to take a moment now and think about whether you know where your limits are in some key areas of life:

- Do you know how much sleep you need each night to feel good and function well?

- Are you aware of which foods make you feel good and which make you wish you had eaten something else?

- Do you know whether you need time with others or by yourself in order to feel energized?

- If you drink, do you know how many alcoholic beverages it takes to cross the line from "enjoyable" to "hangover"?

- Do you have a sense of how many different obligations you can realistically handle?

Most people have at least some idea of the answers to those questions but choose not to do what would be best for them. Common reasons include not wanting to hurt other people's feelings, a sense of obligation, or the belief that if they don't do the task at hand, no one else will. I could ask, "What makes you so special that you can ignore your limits?" But perhaps the better question would be "Why don't you feel that you're special enough that you deserve to respect your limits?"

That's a tough question, and many people struggle to answer it. Regardless of whether or how you answer it, bear in mind that if you don't respect yourself, it's hard for others to respect you. Plus, people generally have more respect for those who care for themselves than those who don't. After all, people who don't take care of themselves tend to be grumpy and not fun to be around because they're burned-out.

If you still feel reluctant, consider this: If others see you taking care of yourself and balancing your time between play and work, they might be inspired to take better care of themselves. That said, this shouldn't be your primary motivation. Self-care is, by definition, about you, not about what you can do for others. You're doing enough of that already. If others are inspired, that's a bonus, but it isn't the goal.

EXERCISE: Self-Care Assessment

This exercise will help you assess where you're already doing a good job in caring for yourself and where there's room for improvement. I'm going to ask you to rate how frequently you engage in self-care in various parts of your life: physical, mental, emotional, spiritual, in relationships, and in the workplace. These lists of self-care activities aren't exhaustive, but they should give you a clearer perspective on whether you're taking good care of yourself, along with ideas about additional self-care activities you might engage in.

Rate each item listed using the following scale:

3 = I do this frequently

2 = I do this occasionally

1 = I rarely do this

0 = I never do this

? = Doing this never occurred to me

Physical Self-Care

_____ *I eat regularly (typically, three meals a day).*

_____ *I eat foods that are healthful.*

_____ *I exercise at least three times a week, for a minimum of thirty minutes each time.*

_____ *I get routine medical checkups.*

_____ *I go to the doctor when I'm sick or injured.*

_____ *I take time off when I'm sick.*

_____ *I get massages or other body treatments, such as manicures or pedicures.*

_____ *I get enough sleep most nights of the week.*

_____ *I engage in sexual activities with my partner or on my own.*

_____ *I wear clothes that I like and that fit well.*

Mental Self-Care

_____ I write in a journal.

_____ I attend individual therapy or support group sessions regularly.

_____ I take day trips or mini vacations.

_____ I regularly turn off electronics, such as the phone, television, and computer.

_____ I read books and magazines for fun, not just for work.

_____ I make time for self-reflection.

_____ I do activities where I'm a beginner or novice, instead of a teacher or expert.

_____ I engage in activities where I can be curious, such as going to shows, art exhibits, sports events, or classes.

_____ I say no to extra responsibilities.

_____ I connect regularly with loved ones with whom I can be authentic and safely share my thoughts and feelings.

Emotional Self-Care

_____ I allow myself to feel a range of emotions, including anger, sadness, fear, and frustration.

_____ I allow myself to outwardly express my true emotions.

_____ I say nice things about myself to myself.

_____ I accept compliments from others without discounting myself.

_____ I spend time in the company of people I enjoy.

_____ I limit contact with those who drain me.

_____ I find things and people who make me laugh and enjoy them regularly.

_____ I use my voice to express outrage against injustices and engage in various forms of activism.

_____ I don't allow the negative emotions of those around me to affect my own emotional state.

_____ I'm mindful to watch for things during my day that will lift my mood.

Spiritual Self-Care

_____ I make time for self-reflection.

_____ I participate in rituals that reflect my spiritual beliefs.

_____ I belong to a community that shares my beliefs.

_____ I spend time in nature.

_____ I embrace optimism and hope.

_____ I count my blessings.

_____ I have an awareness of materialism and its role in my life.

_____ I pray.

_____ I meditate.

_____ I read inspirational literature or listen to inspirational music.

Relationship Self-Care

_____ I have regularly scheduled time to be alone with my partner.

_____ I have regularly scheduled time to be with my children.

_____ I check on and visit with extended family members.

_____ I make time to be with friends.

_____ I stay in contact with friends in distant places.

_____ I spend quality time with pets.

_____ I make time to reply to personal letters and phone calls from others.

_____ I ask for help when I need it.

_____ I have a wide social circle.

_____ I share my thoughts and feelings with those whom I trust.

Professional or Workplace Self-Care

_____ I take breaks during the day (for example, eating lunch or taking a short walk).

_____ I arrange my work space so it's comfortable and inviting.

_____ I get to know my coworkers.

_____ I set limits and boundaries with my clients and colleagues.

_____ I have a set time to go home at the end of the day.

_____ I dedicate part of my day to working uninterrupted.

_____ I balance my workload and prioritize.

_____ I get supervision or seek the guidance of a mentor.

_____ I negotiate for my needs (for example, asking for a raise, more vacation time, or a more flexible schedule).

_____ I leave my work at the office.

Now that you've completed the ratings, look for patterns in your responses. Are there areas of your life where you're doing a better job of self-care? Are there areas that need improvement? Take note of where you'd like to improve, but don't view this as another obligation or a sign that you're somehow lacking. The point is to feel better, not to have a perfect score. Focus on solutions and making a commitment to taking better care of yourself. There are several ways you can remind yourself to follow through:

- *Choose one self-care activity and dedicate the month to engaging in it as often as possible. When the month is up, you can continue that activity and begin a new one, or choose a different one to replace what you did the month before.*

- *Post notes in prominent places reminding you to engage in self-care.*

- *Ask supportive friends and family members to either participate in activities with you or remind you that you need to engage in these activities on your own.*

- *Block out times for self-care on your calendar and keep those appointments no matter what comes up.*

- *Pay for a membership at a gym, spa, or other place where you find enjoyment so you'll feel motivated to go to get your money's worth.*

Self-Care Ideas

If I were to tell you that you had the weekend off and could do whatever you wanted, guilt-free, would you know what you wanted to do? All too often, people get stuck in a rut and can't even think of alternative activities that would be enjoyable.

When clients tell me they have no idea what to do for fun, one of the first questions I ask is what they did for fun as a kid. I recommend that you ask yourself the same question. Did you play outside, draw, paint, make models, build Lego creations, dance, put on shows, cook or bake, make videos, play make-believe, participate in sports, or play a musical instrument? Your answer to this question can provide clues about what might be appealing to you now, perhaps in a "grown-up" form. If none of your former interests excite you now, perhaps there were activities you wanted to do as a kid but couldn't. Could you experiment with one of them now? After all, you're an adult and can make your own choices, and there are no rules about how to have fun in the name of self-care.

Also consider what level of activity and engagement you prefer when it comes to self-care. If you have a job that requires you to be around people constantly, you may want to engage in solo activities during your self-care time, such as yoga, walking in the woods, needlework, reading, or meditation. Alternatively, you may find that interacting with others helps you feel refreshed, in which case you might prefer activities like going out to dinner, taking a group fitness class, or attending concerts, sporting events, and festivals. Above all, don't compromise or try to satisfy other people's expectations. Caregiving is hard work, and these self-care activities will help you keep going.

EXERCISE: Identifying Self-Care Activities

Here's a list of self-care activities that many people find enjoyable. Read through it and check off any that sound appealing to you:

_____ *Watching funny movies or television shows*

_____ *Listening to soothing music*

_____ *Taking a long bath or shower*

_____ *Getting a pedicure or manicure*

_____ *Working on a puzzle*

_____ *Getting out in nature*

_____ *Playing with pets*

_____ *Building something by hand*

_____ *Lighting candles*

_____ *Going out for a treat, like ice cream or coffee*

_____ *Reading a book or magazine for pleasure*

_____ *Coloring a picture*

_____ *Planning a vacation*

_____ *Going fishing*

_____ *Praying*

_____ *Writing letters*

_____ *Daydreaming*

_____ *Cooking a meal*

_____ *Window shopping or browsing in a store*

_____ *Writing in a journal*

_____ *Learning a new skill, such as a foreign language, sport, type of dance, or art technique*

_____ *Sleeping in*

_____ *Creating a ritual that you do on a regular basis*

What other ideas come to mind now that you've seen this list? Make a list in the journal you've been using for the writing exercises throughout this book and turn to it any time you feel at a loss about what you can do to take care of yourself.

The Power of the Written Word

Throughout this book, I've included exercises in which I asked you to write in a journal about your thoughts and feelings related to having a partner with anxiety. Hopefully you've been doing those writing exercises. Now I'd like to encourage you to keep a journal after you've finished reading this book. There are many benefits to journaling. Here are just a few:

- A journal provides a safe, private place to express your thoughts and feelings.

- Your journal entries can provide a record of what has happened to help you refresh your memory later.

- You can explore new ideas in writing before trying them out in the real world.

- You can get specific about plans for the future.

Research indicates that journaling also has many benefits for both mental and physical health (Pennebaker 2000). One reason for this may be that people who express their thoughts in writing feel relieved of the burdens of their stresses once they get them out of their head and onto paper. In fact, people who journal regularly tend to have fewer physical symptoms related to stress, are ill less often, and make fewer trips to the doctor (Pennebaker 2000). Who knew putting a pen to paper could be so effective?

There aren't any rules about how to keep a journal or what to write in a journal, and you need not even use a formal journal. The main purpose is simply to have a place to express your true essence. Some people may write many pages every day. Others may prefer to jot short entries occasionally, or even just doodle or use pictures cut from magazines to express their thoughts. Others may make entries in a routine style, such as always recording the weather and highlights of the day. Do whatever works for you. Again, the purpose is to take care of yourself and have a positive experience.

Another option for journaling is an electronic approach. You might even consider blogging. Most blogging sites allow you to set privacy levels. If you're concerned about a family member or someone else finding and reading a physical journal, a blog that's password-protected and not available for others to browse online may be a solution. You could also write in a password-protected file on a computer.

Disclosure

Does this sound familiar? Once again, your partner isn't with you when you show up at a party. People ask where she is, and you wonder, *Do I tell the truth or make up an excuse?* This isn't the first time you've felt that you needed to make an excuse for your partner's absence, and it's getting old.

Deciding whether to be open about your partner's anxiety is a personal decision. Just be aware that if you keep it a secret, not being open and honest can eat away at your self-esteem and leave you feeling isolated. On the other hand, this isn't just about you; your partner is the one who's anxious, and her privacy is at stake.

Although mental illness has received a great deal of media attention, there is still significant stigma around it. And although some people rightfully advocate that mental illness be regarded similarly to any other chronic physical illness, it's not. People still react differently to the news that someone they know has diabetes versus anxiety, even though both illnesses are devastating on many levels.

The truth is, there isn't one right answer to whether to tell others that your partner has anxiety, and no single ideal approach for how to tell them if you decide to do so. And as mentioned, your partner needs to be involved in the decision, since she's the one struggling with anxiety. If she feels differently about appropriate levels of disclosure, the two of you should try to find an acceptable compromise.

Here are some considerations to keep in mind when deciding whether to disclose your partner's illness:

- What is the purpose of disclosing this information?

- What kind of relationship do you have with the person you're telling, and how might that person use the information?

- How might you or your partner benefit by telling this person? What disadvantages might there be?

Regarding the purpose of the disclosure, you may have many valid reasons for wanting to tell others about your partner's anxiety, including wanting support from family and friends, needing an employer to be flexible, or just because it's not your nature to keep secrets. But what if your partner doesn't want family and friends to know? After all, the people you'd like to tell may be her family and friends as well. As mentioned, you'll need to discuss this and find an acceptable compromise. On one hand, your partner has a right to privacy. On the other hand, you have a right to be honest and feel supported.

Explaining why you'd like to tell specific people may help your partner understand your point of view. However, it's important that you remain open to the reasons for your partner's reluctance as well. She may be afraid of judgment, rejection, or mistreatment, and those may also be valid concerns depending on her history with the people you'd like to tell. A possible compromise would be to select one or two people both of you would feel safe sharing this information with, and then slowly expand the circle as your partner gets more comfortable with the information being public.

The second point, what kind of relationship you have with people you're telling and how they might use that information, relates to the first point. For example, your partner may feel less threatened if you want to tell your employer, who doesn't know her, than if you want to tell your partner's historically critical mother or your best friend, who's wonderful but tends to gossip. There may be valid reasons for telling these people. Perhaps your partner's mother visits regularly and might notice a change in your partner's behavior, or maybe you communicate with your best friend daily and he knows something's up. In these situations, there would still be room for compromise. Perhaps you can communicate that something is indeed going on but limit the amount of information disclosed. Or perhaps after discussing it, you'll both agree that keeping quiet is in everyone's best interest.

Finally, taking into consideration what you've decided regarding the purpose of the disclosure and the relationship you have with the person you're considering talking to, what are the benefits and the disadvantages to disclosing this information? Only you and your partner can figure this out, and you may disagree. What's advantageous to you may be problematic for your partner, and vice versa.

It should be obvious by now, but if not, the bottom line is that you and your partner need to discuss any disclosure about her illness and come to an agreement that feels fair to both of you.

Support Groups

People tend to have strong opinions about working in groups. Some love it, and some hate it. People tend to have even stronger opinions about support groups, and they generally fall into the "hate it" side. Here are some reasons I often hear for not participating in support groups:

- *I'm not a "sharing" kind of person.*

- *I don't want others knowing my business.*

- *Support groups are boring or a waste of my time.*

- *I already know what the other group members are going to say.*

- *People who need to attend support groups are losers. I can handle this myself.*

If you fall into that camp, I'd like to encourage you to reconsider. Bear in mind that support groups aren't the same as group therapy. Group therapy is a formal type of treatment for people with similar mental health conditions, led by a trained mental health professional. Support groups, which are often led by laypeople, have a variety of formats. They may be structured and include educational components, or they may be more focused on sharing experiences. Support groups are often geared toward family members of people struggling with an illness, and the loved one typically doesn't attend so that the caregivers will feel freer to express themselves openly.

Unfortunate as it may be, many people experience the same types of problems. Getting them together in groups is an effective way to reach a lot of people in a short amount of time and also provides an opportunity for people to share their experience and help one another. It also helps with isolation, which can be a big issue when you have a partner with a mental illness such as anxiety. Plus, being in a group can provide reassurance about your relationship as you meet others who have faced similar challenges and still have their relationship intact. Hearing about their experiences may provide insight and useful tools for managing your own relationship. Conversely, by sharing your own experiences, you may be able to help someone else.

Support groups can also provide practical tips about how to handle your partner's anxiety and perhaps even information about new treatments that may be available. Members may share resources such as helpful books and articles, as well as recommendations about mental health professionals who are skilled at treating anxiety. To find support groups in your area, try searching online using keywords such as "family support group," "anxiety," and your city. You can also contact local mental health agencies to ask if they offer or know of any programs for partners of people with anxiety.

If you aren't seeing a therapist, a support group can provide an avenue to identifying difficulties you may be struggling with. You may even be able to work through those issues in a support group. On the other hand, once you experience the benefits of having an outlet in which you can process your thoughts and feelings, you may become interested in engaging in individual therapy.

Individual Therapy

People who have a partner with a mental illness often say things like "She's the one with the problem, not me. Why should I go to therapy? Everything will be fine once she gets over the anxiety." However, those people probably aren't reading this book! But you are, and you've made it to the last chapter and are thinking about your own self-care. So here's a suggestion: consider seeing a therapist yourself. Why? Because being a supportive partner to someone with anxiety takes a lot of effort and energy.

You explored some of your feelings about your situation in chapter 3. Working with a trained therapist who can help you wade through those feelings and make sense of them will be even more helpful. Plus, it's likely that your own self-care has gotten pushed to the side as you've focused on helping your partner. The suggestions and exercises in this chapter have probably given you some ideas for how you can recharge your own batteries, but a therapist can make additional suggestions and also offer support and reinforcement as you begin to make changes. And if you're feeling depressed or anxious yourself, your therapist can help you overcome those challenges as well. Finally, having a neutral third party to listen to your concerns and provide validation and feedback can be a tremendous relief.

In case you wonder, therapy need not be a long-term commitment; it can be of very short duration if that's what you prefer. Either way, it's just one more step you can take toward better self-care.

Yes, You Can Say No to Your Partner

Imagine that it's Friday and you've had a long week. You've been looking forward to going out with your partner and friends tonight to kick off the weekend. But when you get home, your partner is obviously feeling anxious and tells you she doesn't want to go.

What do you do? Do you cancel your plans and stay home? Do you try to talk your partner into going? Or do you go alone? Those questions sound simple, but it's not that easy when your partner has anxiety, is it?

When you have a partner with anxiety, you sacrifice a lot. As discussed throughout the book, your partner probably has periods of time when she isn't herself, can't participate in daily activities, has difficulty working, and just generally isn't holding up her end of the relationship bargain. However, given that you've read and worked through this entire book, it seems that you've decided you're going to stay by her side and weather the storms of anxiety with her.

This doesn't have to mean giving up activities that are important to you or letting go of your own dreams. You have the right to live a rich and fulfilling life—not a narrow existence limited by your partner's anxiety. To that end, here are some tips on how you can protect and enhance your own quality of life:

- **Define your boundaries.** You may be doing as much as you can to help your partner weather and overcome her anxiety. If you feel that you should be doing more but know in your heart that you just don't have more to give, honor that reality. Understand and acknowledge your limits and then discuss them with your partner. You need to set clear boundaries about what you can and cannot do for your partner and for the relationship, or you're likely to stretch yourself too thin. That's a path you don't want to take, as it can lead to depression, anger, low self-esteem, addictive behavior, increased stress, and burnout.

- **Give yourself respite.** Recovery from anxiety generally takes a long time; it's a marathon, not a sprint. Most people who run marathons stop for breaks at water stations along the way, and those stations are strategically placed every couple of miles. On the journey to wellness with your partner, you need similar breaks for respite. The form this takes is entirely up to you, with just one guideline: Be sure to take small respite breaks on a regular basis. If you want a longer break every so often, such as a weekend away from your partner, by yourself or with family and friends, that's fine. But in between those longer breaks, continue to schedule smaller, more frequent activities, such as going on a weekly group run with friends, taking a class a couple of nights each week, or scheduling time to engage in a hobby.

- **Understand that your partner can survive without your constant support.** Early in the recovery process, your partner might be feeling helpless, and you may feel unsure about how to help. There's a good chance that your partner isn't so severely compromised by her illness that she needs your attention and support all the time. She may feel that way, and she may make you feel that way. However, she is an adult and probably hasn't forgotten how to attend to the basics of life. Plus, if you don't respond to her every beck and call, she'll learn that she's capable of handling challenging situations, and this will be empowering in the long run. If you can't get past feeling duty-bound to help or feeling guilty if you don't, I recommend that you consider joining a support group or working with a therapist.

- **Find the "yes."** As you work on setting boundaries, giving yourself respite, and not accommodating your partner's every request for your help or support, you'll probably find yourself saying no to your partner more often than you have been. As you do so, look for opportunities to say yes. For example, if you opt to go out with friends on Friday night as planned, without your partner, explain why this is important to you, and say you'll do whatever she wants to do on Saturday. Relationships always involve compromise, and having a partner with anxiety doesn't change that.

What's Next?

No one can force you to do what's in your best interests. It's up to you to make good choices and take care of yourself so you can be at your best for your partner. If you aren't in the habit of putting your own needs first, this is going to be a challenge, but it's also a huge opportunity—and not just for you. Changing your own life for the better will create a ripple effect, benefiting everyone you come into contact with—including your anxious partner.

Now that you've reached the end of this book, take some time to consider what you've learned. We've explored how anxiety has affected your relationship, what typical partner responses to anxiety are, and tools for communicating effectively. You've also learned a variety of techniques to combat anxiety, including acute anxiety and the six anxiety disorders. Hopefully you've also recognized the importance of self-care to support your own well-being amidst the challenges of being in a relationship with an anxious partner. Many of the ideas and techniques presented throughout this book take time and effort to implement, but the end results—less anxiety for your partner and an improved relationship for both of you—are worth it.

Resources

Anxiety

Bassett, Lucinda. 1996. *From Panic to Power: Proven Techniques to Calm Your Anxieties, Conquer Your Fears, and Put You in Control of Your Life.* New York: HarperCollins.

Bourne, Edmund. 2005. *The Anxiety and Phobia Workbook.* Oakland, CA: New Harbinger.

Bourne, Edmund, and Lorna Garano. 2003. *Coping with Anxiety: 10 Simple Ways to Relieve Anxiety, Fear, and Worry.* Oakland, CA: New Harbinger.

Burns, David. 2007. *When Panic Attacks: The New, Drug-Free Anxiety Therapy That Can Change Your Life.* New York: Morgan Road Books.

Butler, Gillian. 2008. *Overcoming Social Anxiety and Shyness: A Self-Help Guide Using Cognitive Behavioral Techniques.* New York: Basic Books.

Daitch, Carolyn. 2011. *Anxiety Disorders: The Go-To Guide for Clients and Therapists.* New York: W. W. Norton.

Foa, Edna, and Reid Wilson. 2001. *Stop Obsessing: How to Overcome Your Obsessions and Compulsions.* New York: Bantam.

Otto, Michael, and Jasper Smits. 2011. *Exercise for Mood and Anxiety: Proven Strategies for Overcoming Depression and Enhancing Well-Being.* New York: Oxford University Press.

Pavilanis, Steve. 2009. *A Life Less Anxious: Freedom from Panic Attacks and Social Anxiety without Drugs or Therapy.* Chicago: Alpen.

Schiraldi, Glenn. 2009. *The Post-Traumatic Stress Disorder Sourcebook: A Guide to Healing, Recovery, and Growth.* New York: McGraw-Hill.

Tolin, David. 2012. *Face Your Fears: A Proven Plan to Beat Anxiety, Panic, Phobias, and Obsessions.* Hoboken, NJ: John Wiley and Sons.

Wehrenberg, Margaret. 2008. *The 10 Best-Ever Anxiety Management Techniques: Understanding How Your Brain Makes You Anxious and What You Can Do to Change It.* New York: W. W. Norton.

Wilson, Kelly, and Troy DuFrene. 2010. *Things Might Go Terribly, Horribly Wrong: A Guide to Life Liberated from Anxiety.* Oakland, CA: New Harbinger.

Wilson, Reid. 1996. *Don't Panic: Taking Control of Anxiety Attacks.* New York: HarperCollins.

Mindfulness

Forsyth, John, and Georg Eifert. 2007. *The Mindfulness and Acceptance Workbook for Anxiety.* Oakland, CA: New Harbinger.

Gunaratana, Bhante Henepola. 2002. *Mindfulness in Plain English.* Somerville, MA: Wisdom Publications.

Kabat-Zinn, Jon. 2005. *Wherever You Go, There You Are: Mindfulness Meditation in Everyday Life.* New York: Hyperion.

Kabat-Zinn, Jon. 2011. *Mindfulness for Beginners: Reclaiming the Present Moment—and Your Life.* Boulder, CO: Sounds True.

Nhat Hanh, Thich. 1992. *Peace Is Every Step: The Path of Mindfulness in Everyday Life.* New York: Bantam.

Orsillo, Susan, and Lizabeth Roemer. 2011. *The Mindful Way Through Anxiety: Break Free from Chronic Worry and Reclaim Your Life.* New York: Guilford Press.

References

American Psychiatric Association. 2000. *Diagnostic and Statistical Manual of Mental Disorders*, 4th edition, text revision. Washington, DC: American Psychiatric Association.

Antonacci, D., E. Davis, R. Bloch, C. Manuel, and S. Saeed. 2010. CAM for your anxious patient: What the evidence says. *Current Psychiatry* 9(10):43–52.

Balch, P. 2006. *Prescription for Nutritional Healing*. New York: Penguin.

Beck, A., and G. Emery. 2005. *Anxiety Disorders and Phobias: A Cognitive Perspective*. With R. Greenberg. Cambridge, MA: Basic Books.

Bourdon, K. H., J. H. Boyd, D. S. Rae, B. J. Burns, J. W. Thompson, and B. Z. Locke. 1988. Gender differences in phobias: Results of the ECA community survey. *Journal of Anxiety Disorders* 2(3):227–241.

Bourne, E. 2005. *The Anxiety and Phobia Workbook*. Oakland, CA: New Harbinger.

Breslau, N. 2002. Gender differences in trauma and posttraumatic stress disorder. *Journal of Gender-Specific Medicine* 5(1):34–40.

Cohen, L., D. Sichel, J. Dimmock, and J. Rosenbaum. 1994. Impact of pregnancy on panic disorder: A case series. *Journal of Clinical Psychiatry* 55(7):284–288.

Eisenberg, M., R. Olson, D. Neumark-Sztainer, M. Story, and L. Bearinger. 2004. Correlations between family meals and psychosocial well-being among adolescents. *Archives of Pediatrics and Adolescent Medicine* 158(8):792–796.

Hartung, R. 2010. Why does anxiety target women more? FSU researcher awarded $1.8M grant to find out. news.fsu.edu/More-FSU-News/News-Archive/2010/September/Why-does-anxiety-target-women-more-FSU-researcher-awarded-1.8M-grant-to-find-out. Accessed June 1, 2012.

Kabat-Zinn, J. 1990. *Full Catastrophe Living: Using the Wisdom of Your Body and Mind to Face Stress, Pain, and Illness.* New York: Random House.

Kessler, R., L. Andrade, R. Bijl, D. Offord, O. Demler, and D. Stein. 2002. The effects of co-morbidity on the onset and persistence of generalized anxiety disorder in the ICPE surveys. *Psychological Medicine* 32(7):1213–1225.

Kessler, R., W. Chiu, O. Demler, and E. Walters. 2005. Prevalence, severity, and comorbidity of twelve-month *DSM-IV* disorders in the National Comorbidity Survey Replication (NCS-R). *Archives of General Psychiatry* 62(6):617–627.

Kessler, R., C. Foster, W. Saunders, and P. Stang. 1995. Social consequences of psychiatric disorders, I: Educational attainment. *American Journal of Psychiatry* 152(7):1026–1032.

Mennin, D., R. Heimberg, C. Turk, and D. Fresco. 2002. Applying an emotion regulation framework to integrative approaches to generalized anxiety disorder. *Clinical Psychology: Science and Practice* 9(1):85–90.

Miller, J., K. Fletcher, and J. Kabat-Zinn. 1995. Three-year follow-up and clinical implications of a mindfulness meditation-based stress reduction intervention in the treatment of anxiety disorders. *General Hospital Psychiatry* 17(3):192–200.

National Association of Cognitive-Behavioral Therapists. 2011. Cognitive-behavioral therapy. http://nacbt.org/whatiscbt.aspx. Accessed June 1, 2012.

National Institute of Mental Health (NIMH). 2009. *Anxiety disorders*. NIH Publication No. 09 3879. Available at www.nimh.nig. gov/health/publications/anxiety-disorders/nimhanxiety.pdf. Accessed September 24, 2012.

Pennebaker, J. 2000. Telling stories: The health benefits of narrative. *Literature and Medicine* 19(1):3–18.

Pigott, T. 1999. Gender differences in the epidemiology and treatment of anxiety disorders. *Journal of Clinical Psychiatry* 60 (suppl 18):4–15.

Robins L. N., and D. A. Regier (eds.). 1991. *Psychiatric Disorders in America: The Epidemiologic Catchment Area Study*. New York: Free Press.

Russell Research. 2004. Generalized anxiety disorder: Its effects on relationships. Unpublished poll results. Washington, DC: Anxiety Disorders Association of America.

Shear, M., M. Cloitre, D. Pine, and J. Ross. 2005. *Anxiety Disorders in Women: Setting a Research Agenda*. Silver Spring, MD: Anxiety Disorders Association of America.

Turgeon, L., A. Marchand, and G. Dupuis. 1998. Clinical features in panic disorder with agoraphobia: A comparison of men and women. *Journal of Anxiety Disorders* 12(6):539–553.

Turner, S., D. Beidel, R. Roberson-Nay, and K. Tervo. 2003. Parenting behaviors in parents with anxiety disorders. *Behaviour Research and Therapy* 41(5):541–554.

Kate N. Thieda, MS, LPCA, NCC, is a licensed professional counselor associate, national certified counselor, and psychotherapist in Durham, North Carolina. She is the creator of the blog *Partners in Wellness* on the award-winning website psychcentral.com, targeted to partners of those who have mental illness. She graduated with her bachelor of arts from Michigan State University and a master of science in counseling from the University of North Carolina at Greensboro.

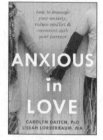